LEGERING

First published in Great Britain in 1993
by Boxtree Limited

1 3 5 7 9 10 8 6 4 2

Edited by Helen Douglas-Cooper
Designed by Anita Ruddell

Colour origination by Fotographics, Hong Kong

Printed and bound in Great Britain by
Butler & Tanner Ltd, Frome and London for
Boxtree Limited
Broadwall House
21 Broadwall
London SE1 9PL

A CIP catalogue entry for this book is available from the British Library.

ISBN 1 85283 188 X

LEGERING

Edited by Mac Campbell
with a foreword by Dick Clegg

BⓈXTREE

A bream safely in the net brings a smile to Dick Clegg's face.

CONTENTS

ACKNOWLEDGEMENTS 6

FOREWORD 7

INTRODUCTION 9

CHAPTER 1
THE BASICS 11

CHAPTER 2
THE QUIVERTIP 29

CHAPTER 3
THE SWINGTIP 36

CHAPTER 4
BUTT INDICATORS 46

CHAPTER 5
SLACKLINING AND OTHER METHODS 53

CHAPTER 6
END RIGS AND KNOTS 61

CHAPTER 7
TIGHTENING AND TWITCHING 74

CHAPTER 8
LEGERING FOR BREAM 84

CHAPTER 9
THE OPEN-ENDED SWIMFEEDER 94

CHAPTER 10
BLOCK-END FEEDERS 112

CHAPTER 11
BAITS AND GROUNDBAITS 133

INDEX 143

ACKNOWLEDGEMENTS

The editor and publishers would like to thank the following:
Malcolm Lane for use of his illustrations
Bob Atkins, Angus Murray and Matthew Roberts for use of their
photographs.

Thanks also to all of the anglers who have helped to contribute to
Improve Your Coarse Fishing magazine since its launch in 1991.

FOREWORD

There have been hundreds of books published about fishing generally, about catching big fish of all species, about floatfishing and about pole fishing. However, I can't think of one that has been exclusively about legering, and this is an astonishing omission when you consider that more big fish are caught on leger tackle in this country than by all other methods put together.

There are many anglers who won't leger because they dare not try something different, while others simply like watching a float. And, inevitably, there are some who have tried legering but not had much success because they weren't doing it properly. I have been in the tackle trade for much of my working life – first as a tackle dealer and now as a tackle wholesaler – and my heart bleeds for all those anglers who do their best but who don't get results, because I know how much effort some of them put in. Yet all of us, when we tackle something new, need help, whether it's in the form of advice from friends, magazines or books, that's how I learned. So I welcome this book in particular, as it is filling a huge gap in the market. And if it introduces just a few anglers to the basics of legering I will be a very happy man.

As I write this I have just returned from the World Championships in Ireland – an event in which legering is banned. And I can safely say without any fear of contradiction that if legering had been allowed in this match the anglers would have caught many times more fish than they eventually did. That's how good legering is when conditions are difficult.

Having said that, I must point out that I am not, in fact, in favour of allowing legering in this particular event, because it would greatly reduce the spectator-appeal. And many Continental countries ban legering in their matches, so it would be grossly unfair on many teams.

As a specimen hunter before I became a matchman – and later manager of the England team – I know just how many advantages legering (and I include swimfeedering) can give anglers of all abilities, from the rank novice to the very experienced, on both still and running water. It's a method no-one should be ignoring, for it will catch you fish – and lots of them – when floatfishing is out of the question because of either the conditions or the sheer casting distance involved. Yet it is also a winner at times in conditions that are perfect for floatfishing. And because of this I urge you not to fall into the trap of becoming addicted to legering just because it's easy – for it will ruin your enjoyment of fishing. The leger man who ignores other methods will miss out on as much pleasure as the float angler who ignores legering. Treat it as just another weapon in your armoury, to be used only when it is definitely the best method at your disposal.

Frankly, I wish a book like this had been available when I

started fishing. It would have saved me many hours of heartbreak and unsuccessful experiments. My advice is to read it and adapt the ideas for your own waters. Some will work; others might not. However it can't fail to start you on the right road if you have never legered, or to give you plenty of ideas if you're already experienced at it.

Good luck, and tight lines!

Dick Clegg
Manager of England World Championship Team

A beautiful day, and a barbel caught on leger tackle. What more could an angler wish for?

LEGERING ADVANTAGES

The lure of the float has a lot to answer for, because the sight of that red tip slowly sinking below the surface still sets most anglers' hearts beating just that little bit faster. In that fraction of a second the same scenario flies through the angler's mind – the strike, a satisfying thump-thump, and somewhere down in the depths a fish strains for its freedom. If there's a more thrilling moment in fishing, I have yet to experience it.

So why leger?

The answer is simple – legering catches fish. And quite often it will catch you more fish than a float would. The pity is that floatfishing is just so exciting, bringing back memories of those small perch we caught beside lock gates when we were kids; of little, suicidal roach that just refused to stop feeding as the sun set; or of big, brown tench that made off with our bait on those shimmering summer days when nothing else would feed. The float stirs old memories that keep flitting across my mind, and I wouldn't have it any other way.

Yet legering has accounted for many more of my good fish than floatfishing ever did. And if you speak to anglers who specialise in catching big fish they will tell you the same thing. Because when your quarry is 40 or 50 yd away in the middle of a lake, or when there's a strong wind blowing which makes floatfishing all but impossible, you have two choices – to go home; or put up a leger rig.

Up to the 1960s, however, there was hardly a mention of legering in most angling books, for it was regarded as a 'specialist' method. For example, *Bream Fishing* by Peter Tombleson, published in the early 1950s, devotes about 300 words to the subject.

How different now, when almost every successful angler in the country regards legering as another weapon in his armoury – and a very effective weapon, too. No longer is legering regarded as a lazy man's way of fishing, though to be honest, it's certainly the easiest way of getting a bait out to the

9

fish. And if I had to bet on which method produced the most really big fish for the 'ordinary' angler my money would go on the leger.

Neither is legering any less exciting than floatfishing. In fact after many thousands of trips legering for bream on my local Fen drains I really think that the sight of a swingtip slowly lifting as the line cuts through the waves on a warm, overcast summer's evening, is just as exciting as watching a float. For one thing it can take several seconds, which does the old heart no good at all when you've just seen bream wallowing about on the surface above your groundbait. And you have to sit on your trembling hands to prevent yourself striking too soon.

Regular carp anglers know the feeling – at night their best chance of a fish is to leger, with an electronic bite indicator, which will flash, or buzz, or both, when they get a bite. Legering, to these anglers, is a way of life. They experiment with leger weights, spend hours modifying their bite alarms, and even go out practising their casting techniques. They do it because legering catches them fish! Pike anglers also leger. Spinning may be more enjoyable on a winter's morning when the frost scrunches beneath your feet and a warm fire beckons after a three-hour session among the small jack pike. However, the average angler knows that his best chance of a really big fish lies in getting a bait right into the required spot and making it stay there. If livebaiting is not allowed – and there are more and more waters where it is banned – then a big deadbait is the answer. Legered, of course.

However, this is not a book only about catching big fish on a leger. It is for the average angler who wants to see what other anglers do, how they fish, and what they catch. Many's the time when match anglers will catch fish of ½ oz or less, one after the other, on a leger because floatfishing is out of the question, or because legering is getting them more bites. There are plenty of times when a leger angler, sitting beside a float angler, and putting his bait the same distance from the bank, will catch more fish.

Gone are the times when you leger only because you can't catch fish on a float. The modern angler has a choice of many methods – floatfishing with rod and line, floatfishing with a pole, freelining (with no weight at all on the line), flyfishing or legering. And of all the methods used to catch coarse fish, legering is the easiest. It's also the most under-used method with the average angler, and with many top-class anglers, including matchmen, who insist on watching their float ride the waves, even though they're not catching anything, when they should change to a leger. I know this is so – I sometimes do it myself. That old, favourite float has a lot to answer for!

THE BASICS

Legering involves having a weight on the end of your line to hold the tackle in place, as opposed to a float rig, which is likely to move around a swim with the flow, or be blown about by the wind. Of course, floatfishing with a weight on the bottom is almost a form of legering. However, for our purposes the leger weight is not tied directly on to the line – and the fish is able to make off with the bait without feeling the weight.

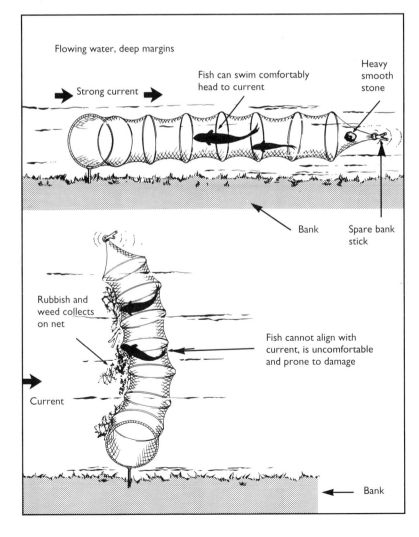

Flowing water, deep margins

Strong current

Fish can swim comfortably head to current

Heavy smooth stone

Bank

Spare bank stick

Rubbish and weed collects on net

Current

Fish cannot align with current, is uncomfortable and prone to damage

Bank

Your first consideration must always be for the fish. In stillwaters the net must not be allowed to collapse and must be pegged out if necessary. In fast waters the net must always be placed parallel with the bank, as shown, and pegged very securely with a bank stick or sticks through the ring at the end. A large stone can help anchor it to the bottom...but remember it's there when you release the fish.

11

This is achieved in one of many ways. The simplest (and perhaps the best-known, certainly among anglers who were fishing 40 years ago) is a drilled bullet. The line is threaded through the bullet, and stopped from sliding down to the hook by a split shot. When a fish picks up the bait it swims off, pulling the line through the bullet, which remains in place on the lake or river bed.

It doesn't matter very much how big the leger weight is. In fact there's a good argument for making it big, so that at whatever angle the fish swims away, the bullet stays where it is. A very small bullet, not much bigger than a split shot, can move when the fish pulls the line, putting pressure on the line that the fish will feel. And then there's the danger of it dropping the bait.

Seeing your bites

This is the part that puts a lot of anglers off legering – they don't think they are going to see a bite. By far the best solution is to ask a well-known angler to take you fishing in a place where he would leger and show you how to do it. Sit beside him and do what he does. I did this many years ago with National Angling Champion Bryan Lakey. He fixed me up with a swingtip, and I was still dubious. In the wind it seemed to have a life of its own, blowing this way and that for about half an hour; and I began to get discouraged. However he encouraged me not to give up, and I left my own rod and looked at his.

His swingtip was also waving around. Then suddenly it went out straight. Without doubt it was a bite, and in fact he struck and hooked a small bream. I couldn't believe that the bite was so positive – I had been looking for little twitches. I went back to my own rod knowing at last what I was looking for, and within another 15 minutes I had my first fish on leger tackle – a nice roach.

There are many ways of spotting bites. As with float tackle, the fish moves the line, and you have some sort of implement near the rod to help you spot the bite. And, despite what may turn out to be a travesty of description on my part, they all work. If they didn't anglers wouldn't use them!

Advantages and disadvantages of legering

I will stick my neck out and say that every angler who has never legered would catch more fish if he learned how to leger. The advantages are:
  • Casting is easier and more accurate, with fewer false casts.
  • You can fish swims that are too far away to cast a float to.
  • You can fish on windy days when floatfishing is out of the

Legering will allow you to cast to fish which are out of floatfishing range.

question.
- The rigs are less complicated than with ordinary float tackle.
- You don't have to plumb the depth.
- Legering will hold a bait in the required spot.
- It presents the still (or almost-still) bait that larger specimens so often prefer.

Against these, you need to weigh the following disadvantages:
- On a bottom that is heavily weeded, legering can be almost impossible – although specimen hunters have devised ingenious methods of getting over this problem.
- It is not possible to present a bait at one level off the bottom, as it is with float tackle.
- You need a proper leger rod, though legering is possible with a float rod. In fact the first time I ever legered in a match I used a float rod and won the event with more than 20 lb of bream. It's not to be advised, however, except in an emergency.

13

What you can catch

There's not a fish swimming that can't be caught on leger tackle. You can even, with very little preparation, catch fish on the surface provided the water is no more than about 6 ft deep. Indeed, Bob Nudd, the Englishman who became the first man to win the World Championship two years in a row, catches lots of carp from the surface using the simplest of leger rigs together with floating maggots. It's so exciting – you can see where the carp are boiling, cast a leger weight to them, and see them take your bait from the surface.

Of all the fish that fall to a legered bait, perhaps it's the bream which, until recently, has had the most publicity. And since the Boston, Lincs, angler Jack Clayton revolutionised legering in the 1950s with his invention of the swingtip, legering has become the most popular method of catching bream, on stillwaters and rivers alike. This method will be described later – the swingtip screws into a special threaded end ring with which most leger rods are already fitted, and hangs down from the tip of the rod. More than one angler on seeing it for the first time has said: 'I see you've broken your rod end'. But it's very effective, and easy to use.

Legering is now the standard method for catching specimen carp. Every weekend throughout the summer and autumn, and even frequently in the winter, thousands of anglers spend the night waiting for their electronic bite alarms to tell them that, far out in the lake, a huge fish has taken their bait. Then can follow the battle of a lifetime with a carp of 30 lb or more. Legering gets the bait out to where these huge fish patrol their beats – no other method could do that. And these fanatical anglers have refined the method almost to a fine art, with special hooks, rigs, reels and rods.

If you substitute the leger weight for a swimfeeder you don't even have to worry about getting the bait out to the fish – the swimfeeder does it for you. Small wonder that this is now probably the most popular variation of legering in the UK – and so effective that some match anglers believe it should be banned on some waters because it's so easy!

Rods

Thirty years ago, the typical leger rod was a cut-down float rod with an extra-strong tip, used with very crude, heavy tackle. Modern rods are far better designed. They can be split roughly into three types – the general-purpose leger rod, the swimfeeder rod and the specimen, carp or pike rod. Unless you know exactly what you are looking for, avoid the 'fishing kits' sold in toy shops and supermarkets. There may be some bargains here, but I've never seen one.

Get your first proper rod from a proper tackle dealer, or get a secondhand one from a mate if you're sure that what you are buying is what you want. A good tackle dealer is worth his weight in gold – his information is free and it's not in his interest to sell you a rod not suited to your type of fishing, because he wants you back to his shop over the coming weeks, spending money on bait and other accessories. Ideally take an experienced angler along for a second opinion; then at least you'll know you've come out equipped with some decent tackle.

General-purpose leger rods

While the use of carbon has transformed rod design in the last few years, making them much slimmer and lighter than previously, this is one area in which the average angler will gain less advantage from using a carbon rod than in most others. If you can afford one, then get it – they really are a delight to use. However, plenty of good anglers happily use 15-year-old glassfibre models, because they have a most pleasant and forgiving action.

There is, however, a warning you should heed. The modern carbon specialist light leger rod probably has a slim tip specially designed to absorb a strike against a good fish while light lines are being used. And it's possible to use hook lengths as low as 1 lb or even 12 oz with these tools. Many glassfibre rods were, however, designed in an era when such fine lines were not in general use, and unless you are very experienced, and know the limitations of the rod well, you will have to use hook lengths of around 2 lb or more if you are to avoid breaking on the strike. It was with such a rod that I caught 20 bream weighing almost 100 lb to break the Middle Level System match record. It was a Ken Smith swingtip, named after a former National Champion, and was at least 20 years old. I used it with 1½ lb breaking strain line as a hook bottom, which is less than I would recommend, but it is an exceptionally soft rod. There are still glassfibre rods being marketed, some of them with a carbon tip, that gives you the best of both worlds – sensitivity and 'give' on the strike and that lovely 'feel' down the rod when you are playing a fish. In addition, they are cheaper than carbon models.

Your final choice largely depends on the areas you fish. If you have to tempt your fish from clear-water canals, when fine lines are necessary even to get a bite, you must go for a rod that will handle 12-oz bottoms (the popular name for hook lengths). The specifications of the rod should make it clear that it is for this type of light work. It will probably be on the short side – perhaps 6–8 ft, because the fish will be at fairly close range – and will certainly have a spliced or very

15

Above: most leger rods come fitted with a threaded end ring.

Right: for canal fishing rods are light and slim.

light tip that is soft in the first 12 in or so. This absorbs the strike and prevents the light line from breaking.

If your fishing is done at long range on stillwaters, for fair-sized fish like tench, bream and small carp, you will need a rod capable of picking up a lot of line. It will need to be up to ten ft in length, perhaps longer, and have much more of an 'all-through' action, with bags of give in it if you overstrike. And you will be using hook lengths of around 2 lb minimum, since with anything less than that you can easily break on the strike, especially if a big fish is moving away from you at speed.

Most general-purpose leger rods come equipped with a threaded tip ring that will take a screw-in swingtip or a quivertip, to help you see your bites. Some models also come

16

with a choice of top joints, which will enable you to use the rod with a much greater variety of line strengths or leger weights. And some quivertip rods come with a choice of top joints each fitted with a different strength quivertip. These are particularly useful to the angler who does a fair amount of legering.

There is also a type of rod known as a 'wand' or 'winklepicker'. This is a type of quivertip rod, around 6½ ft long or less, and is useful for tucking into the bank on windy days, or for using in heavily-reeded waters where the vegetation makes it difficult to position a longer rod sideways to the water.

Swimfeeder rods

A swimfeeder is an attachment that takes the place of a leger weight. It is hollow, and will hold maggots or other pieces of bait. A small one may weigh little more than a leger weight, and can be fished using a normal leger rod. On fast waters such as the River Severn, or where a lot of line is left between rod and swimfeeder on a moving water such as the River

A powerful swimfeeder rod in action.

Trent, a considerable weight may be needed – as much as 3 oz or more. A normal rod would not be capable of casting such a weight, nor of striking into a big fish with the extra weight on the tackle, so a stiffer and stronger rod is needed.

There is a wide range of swimfeeder rods on the market, and if you are using a swimfeeder with more than about ½ oz of weight attached, you will definitely benefit from getting one. The modern, specially-designed models are capable of handling an amazing range of weights, and some have a choice of two or more tips, which will handle almost any situation you are likely to come across in the UK. If, however, you can afford to get two rods, go for a lightish one about 10 ft long and a stronger one at 12 ft. The light ones are sometimes described as 'Quiver/Light feeder', and will probably be used with lines of 3 lb to 4 lb, while the heavier ones will handle lines from 4 lb up to the 8 lb you'll need if you're continually hurling out a 4-oz feeder and hooking barbel or big chub in fast water.

A specialist swimfeeder rod will have a tip on which the bite will register – the principle is covered more fully later – but in fast water this is not the main thing to look for; your first job is to get the feeder out to your chosen spot. I have a feeder rod with interchangeable top joints, and the first time I used it I chose the finer tip for fishing with a 4-oz feeder on a fast stretch of the Trent. Before the day was out the top 2 in of the tip had broken off! It was entirely my fault. Casting the swimfeeder out about once a minute for six hours, and then retrieving in the fast water, often with a fish on, put the tip under a strain it had not been designed for. I have fished that place several times since, and have always used the stronger tip, with no trouble at all – I can still see the bites.

Specimen and specialist rods

If you're going to concentrate on catching just big fish you'll need a specialist rod of some sort. You can land big fish on normal, all-round leger rods, but you may need a bit of luck and it may take you a long time. With a more powerful rod you can use – indeed you must use – a stronger line, and the combination will enable you to land the fish more quickly than on 'average' tackle. So the man after big carp, pike, bream, chub, barbel or tench will do well to get himself a rod capable of handling these fish. Generally the rods have a quoted 'test curve'. This has nothing do do with the strength of line you should use, but is an indication of the amount of pull needed to bend the rod so that the tip is at right-angles to the butt.

Test curves for these special rods will normally be between 1¾ lb and about 4½ lb. And as a general guide the strength of line to use is about five times the quoted test curve. So with a 2 lb test-curve rod you would be expecting to use approximately a 10-lb line. Of course the size of hook needed is normally greater than that for general fishing – and this fact alone means that you must have more powerful gear. It's a question of balancing everything up, which is not difficult and comes with experience.

The principle – and this applies to all fishing – is that it takes more pressure to pull a large hook into a fish than it does a small hook. The large hook requires the angler to use stronger line, since light line would snap before the necessary pressure was exerted. And to get the maximum pressure on the strong line you need a more powerful rod. A small hook and light line needs only a light pressure to pull it into the fish, so a light rod is sufficient, and a stronger rod would cause the light line to break long before the rod started to bend properly.

As with general-purpose rods, modern specialist rods are generally very good indeed, and you can hardly go wrong if you buy a recognised brand. The best source of information is from adverts in angling magazines. These adverts give all sorts of information, and there are some one-man firms who will build a rod to your own specifications – even down to the colour of the whippings and with your own name on the butt. The men who make these custom-built rods are all anglers themselves, and really know their business If you have the money to buy these top-line rods you know you're getting the very best.

Reels

For all forms of legering there's only one type of reel to consider: the fixed-spool, so called because the spool remains fixed and an arm winds the line back on when you retrieve. Line spills off the end when you cast, in the same way that cotton pulls off a cotton reel. There are two main types: the standard spool, which has the base of the spool inside the main body of the reel; and the skirted spool, which has the spool overlapping the body. The tendency now is to go for the skirted spools, as it is possible for a fine line to be blown into the gap between the body and spool on the normal fixed-spool; this is virtually impossible with a skirted spool. It doesn't happen very often with the normal one, though, and if in doubt you should choose whichever one you feel happiest with.

All fixed-spool reels have a bale arm that has to be clicked back for casting and put back into place afterwards. A turn of the handle does this. Some anglers prefer the automatic type, however, which allows you to touch the bale arm with your

19

Above: left, a normal open-faced fixed-spool; right, a skirted spool model.

Above right: when using an automatic reel always leave the bale arm hanging downwards, so you don't accidentally touch it and flick it open on the strike.

finger as you cast, when it flies open. Then you turn the handle, as with other models, to get it back into position. These are very popular with match anglers, since it allows one-handed operation and is marginally quicker than using a reel without this facility. There's no reason why non-match anglers shouldn't consider getting one. They are a bit more expensive, of course, and generally it's only the top-line models which have this facility. For heavy swimfeedering you should not use the automatic operation even if it's on your reel because the continual strain of casting the heavy weight can quickly ruin the mechanism. You should use the reel as you would a manual model, and hold the line in your crooked finger to cast.

If you do use an automatic fixed-spool there is one minor problem when legering. When you grab the rod and strike, your finger can hit the bale arm, which springs open and will probably lose you the fish. The answer is to position the arm so that it is under the spool. The top of the spool, which is close to your fingers when you grab the rod, is clear. I have hit the bale arm many times, I have to admit, and lost fish because of it. But I still prefer the automatic reel for all my fishing except trotting a float down a moving river, when I always opt for a closed-face reel. These are designed to take light lines and to allow the angler to fish with the spool open and then to close it when a fish is on without the horrible pause you can get with open-faced, fixed-spool reels. I have seen anglers legering using a closed-face reel, but I would not advise it unless you have no other model handy.

There's a wide range of modern fixed-spools, costing from just £5 or £6 up to £50 or more. A cheap model will probably do the job sufficiently well for at least a few months, but if you can afford a good one, get it as it will last for many years and be cheaper in the long run. Your choice will depend largely on your pocket, though you must make some attempt to balance the size and weight of the reel to the rod. And if you're going after specimen fish you must be prepared to pay

20

a reasonable amount as using a cheap reel is asking for trouble when you hook your first big fish. In these circumstances it's the gearing that can let you down. The average angler may have little trouble from reels seizing up, but the specimen hunter is putting his gear under a lot more pressure.

Advice from angling friends or the tackle dealer is invaluable here. And you should also take into account that the well-known brands can be repaired and serviced, since there will be spares available from tackle dealers or the UK factory. Buying a brand no-one has heard of is asking for trouble – where do you get the spare parts? You'll need spares eventually, since reels contain moving parts and, like cars, bits wear out and perish. Even so the longevity of quality reels is astounding. I have two Mitchell Otomatics, with automatic bale arms, which I bought more than 20 years ago, and they were secondhand then! They've been away a couple of times to the manufacturer for servicing (they should have been serviced every year, really) and, though definitely not as good as new, they have served me in good stead for far longer than I deserve.

Legering a static bait in winter allows you to keep your hands in your pockets! But it also catches fish!

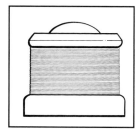

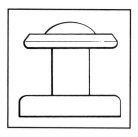

Most fixed-spool reels come with a deep spool (top). They must be filled so that your line comes to within ⅛ in of the top lip (bottom). If necessary use thick nylon or even string to bulk out the spool, then wind 100 yards of your own line on top.

The best tip of all

Without any doubt the best single tip it is possible to give an angler using a fixed-spool reel is to ensure that it is correctly filled. The line level should be kept to within about ⅛ in of the lip of the spool, and there must not be a knot in it. The models that have a special 'match' spool are perfect. A short length of line, perhaps 50 or 100 yd, will fill these to just the right level, and casting will be a dream.

If a spool is underfilled it will cut down your distance to less than half of what it should be, and all anglers should carry a quantity of spare reel line to keep it up to the correct level. So unless you're into specimen fishing you would be well advised to try to get a shallow spool. In all cases, if you are not sure how much line to put on, ask an experienced angler to fill it for you. Also beware of those knots – don't have them at any price. Even if properly tied they will almost certainly reduce the length of your cast – you'll see a definite jerk in mid-cast. And at worst they could cost you the fish of a lifetime.

If you can afford it, you should also get at least one spare spool for your reel, and preferably more. Then if you lose line or have a problem, you are not tempted to soldier on – you can just change spools. It's also essential to have a selection of line strengths, particularly if you have a float rod as well, as most anglers will. You can leger or floatfish at short range with 2-lb line, but for long-range waggler or leger fishing you'll need at least 3 lb. And for swimfeeder fishing in even medium-paced water you may need 4 lb or more. You should also have spares of each of the main strengths you carry. I have about eight spools, including one carrying 8 lb for the odd occasion when I find myself trying to catch carp or pike.

Lines

A table giving approximate minimum strengths of reel line needed for different jobs will help the newcomer:

Light legering for small fish at short range, up to 15 yd	2 lb
Light legering up to 15 yd for medium fish, 1 lb-plus	2½ lb
Legering up to 30 yd for small or medium fish	3 lb
Legering beyond 30 yd or for fish 3 lb-plus	4 lb
Casting ½ oz weight	3 lb
Casting 1 oz weight	4 lb
Casting heavy swimfeeder over 2 oz	5 lb
Fishing for big tench, carp, pike, catfish or barbel	8 lb

Don't forget that most of the time you will be using a hook length that is less than the reel-line strength. Also the reel line takes a lot of battering, rubbing on the bottom and shooting through rod rings, so you have to assume it is going to lose some of its strength after a short while. Lines below 2 lb are so light, and blow about in the wind so much, that it is not really practical to use them as reel line. Stick to 2 lb minimum, and err on the heavy side to be safe.

The important point is that the rod should also be matched to the line. Hooking a big carp on strong line will do you no good at all if you have only a light leger rod that bends double every time you put strain on it. Of course, conditions dictate your tackle. It is possible for a very experienced match angler to land big fish, given a bit of luck, on light tackle if there are no snags around, though he will need to have his hook and line strength balanced to the rod. However, the best angler in the world will never manage it if the fish dives straight into a snag.

As you become more experienced you will find that occasionally you can drop the line strengths given provided you have a rod with an action capable of both handling the hook length you are using and casting the weight you need.

You should renew all nylon lines from time to time. Sunlight is the worst enemy, so the person who fishes several times a week may renew most of his lines every few weeks. The average angler should certainly put new lines on once each season, and especially those lines of 3 lb or less. However, a line that has been used for several trips is likely to be a good line for legering because it will tend to sink, and 99 times out of 100 you will want the line to sink as easily as possible. This is particularly important if you're using a light weight and want to sink the line without moving the bait out of position.

Washing-up liquid on the line, applied by running it through a sponge containing the liquid when you retrieve also helps take away the grease that causes lines to float. Some spare spools come in a plastic case that can be filled with warm, diluted washing-up liquid, which is excellent for getting the line to sink, before you leave home. Of course, the whole spool – including the centre hole – becomes filled with the liquid, but mine never come to any harm. You can treat any spool in a similar way by putting it in a polythene bag containing diluted washing-up liquid. Be warned, though, that this treatment causes nylon to lose its strength, so lines treated like this should be checked frequently.

For rod-and-line and pole anglers the diameter of the line is usually the first thing they check, rather than just the breaking strain. However, there is a pitfall here for the leger angler. You will see a lot in angling magazines about modern Hi-tec

Soaking the spool and line in washing-up liquid is the best way of ensuring your line sinks in use.

23

lines. These have a smaller diameter for their strength than standard lines, and have been pre-stretched in order to achieve this. So while a scientific test will show that they are as strong as other lines at breaking point, they are likely to reach the breaking point more quickly. For the pole angler, who is fishing with a light flick tip or elastic at the tip of his pole, this poses no problem. His smaller-diameter nylon may well get him more bites, and allow the bait to be presented better, and he has the elastic as a considerable buffer if he hits a big fish. The float angler may also find it some advantage. However, for the leger angler it is decidedly dodgy, because it is the stretch in the nylon which is the buffer when you hit a big fish steaming off in the other direction. So steer away from Hi-tec lines for legering, for both hook lengths and reel lines. When you are very experienced you may decide that occasionally the risk is worth it, but I never have!

Leger weights

By far the most popular leger weight in the UK is the Arlesey bomb, the pear-shaped weight designed by the late Dick Walker for use in Arlesey Lake, Bedfordshire, and named after it. The streamlined shape gives it a wobble-free flight in the air and it enters the water without too much of a splash. The old Arlesey bombs were made from lead, which is now banned for leger weights of less than 1 oz, and were often hammered flat to grip the bottom better in moving water. It's not so easy to flatten the new, non-toxic weights, because they are made from harder material. However, some enterprising firms have come up with Arlesey-bomb-shaped

Leger weights.
Top row: normal non-toxic Arlesey bombs (the shiny one should be painted black).
Bottom row: Dexter interchangeable weights, which allow you to screw different-sized weights into the same head.

weights that have been moulded with flattened edges, and these work extremely well.

The Dexter weight is a useful item. The threaded top part can be left tied to the line and the bodies interchanged. Originally cylindrical in shape, which made quite a splash when they hit the water, they now come in the same shape as an Arlesey bomb, in a nice, dull brown colour.

Although all the new non-toxic weights are less shiny than those made of lead, some anglers still camouflage them by painting them with a dark matt paint, so they are not so conspicuous under water. Bream anglers are the most fussy about this, as this species is most easily frightened, though the specialist carp anglers also sometimes paint their leger weights. Carp anglers also have a range of variations on the Arlesey bomb theme, with lengths of long tubing attached to the eye. These weights often have a mechanism that causes the tubing to stand up when on the lake bed, raising the reel line above any bottom weed. These are all on sale in tackle shops that specialise in carp rigs – usually those with a specimen carp water nearby – and from mail-order outlets. There are even whole books written on rigs for carp, and readers interested in this aspect of the sport would do well do get themselves one.

Forged hooks are stronger, but thick in the wire.

Hooks

Modern hooks are, on the whole, well made, though it is as well to check that the point has not been blunted before you use one. Usually you can tell if it is, because when you come to hook a maggot its skin feels extra hard. That hook is of no use, and should be changed. One England International throws away more than half the hooks he buys because they do not reach his exacting requirements. That may sound drastic, but it is not unusual to find a packet containing several obviously blunt samples. It is never worth using a suspect hook, because they are so cheap and provide your main contact with the fish.

As to patterns, most anglers end up with favourite patterns for different jobs. Angling magazines frequently quote top match and carp anglers stating the hooks they use. You can't go far wrong following their advice. What is more important, however, is that you should understand the difference between a forged hook and a fine-wire hook. The forged hook is very much tougher, but the wire is thicker. If you are using a very small bait like a single maggot or a single caster the forged hook affects its natural sink rate considerably. It can also burst a maggot or a caster, whereas a fine-wire hook will not do so. This creates something of a dilemma for the angler with good fish in his swim.

25

My basic rule of thumb is to use a forged hook when legering if I have a reasonable expectation of hooking something decent – say 2 lb or over. If my chances of doing that are small, and if I am struggling and need to use a tiny bait, then I'll take a chance. So my wallet contains fine-wire hooks in 16 and 18 for casters (these have long shanks which makes it easier to bury a hook in a caster), and in sizes 20, 22, 24 and 26 for use with hook maggots, pinkies or squatts. However, I rarely would consider going down to a hook smaller than a size 22 when legering, even at short range in winter.

My forged hooks are from size 22 up to size 2 (the bigger sizes for luncheon meat or sweetcorn). And all-round, the sizes I use most when legering in matches are 18 and 20. For pleasure fishing where I expect better fish I would go straight on to a size 14 or 12.

Your hook length must always be matched to your choice of hook. This is most important when using sizes above about 16, because the pressure you exert must be sufficient to set the hook in the fish without the line breaking. Try to set a size 2 hook into a barbel with 1 lb line and you can imagine the result – snap! It is not physically possible – a size 2 hook needs more pressure to drive it in up to the barb than does a size 22. A table is useful, ignore it at your peril:

Sizes 22, 20 minimum	1 lb line
Size 18, minimum	1½ lb
Sizes 16, 14, minimum	2 lb
Sizes 12, 10, 8, minimum	3 lb
Above that, minimum	4 lb

A size 20 hook on a 2-lb hook length is perfectly all right so far as strength is concerned. So always err on the side of extra line strength for your hook length. Nine times out of ten I start with a 1½ lb hook length, even if I start on a size 20, which is my favourite starting size. It allows me to drop or increase a size with no problems.

There are also all sorts of hook patterns – long-shank, medium-shank and (these are difficult to find now) short-shank. In fact, modern short-shanked hooks almost all have much longer shanks than short-shanked hooks did 20 years ago, which is annoying because unless I am using a single caster on a hook I like to use a short shank. Less metal shows than with a longer shank, and it weighs less, and both considerations are likely to get me more bites. However, the choice is yours, as is the colour. I prefer a blued or a black hook, as it is less likely to flash in the water.

26

Recently there has been a swing to barbless hooks. Indeed some waters ban barbed hooks. This is because inexperienced anglers find barbless hooks easier to remove, and so cause the fish little damage. And provided you keep a tight line to a fish you are not likely to lose many more than if you use a barbed hook. Pole anglers, though, can lose a lot of fish if they have to let the line go slack as they break down their pole. And leger anglers also have a problem – it is almost impossible to leger a worm on a barbless hook, as the worm will slide off very quickly. You will also find it difficult to leger maggots on a barbless hook. When I'm fishing a 'barbless-only' water I cram three or four on and hope that a couple stay put long enough for a fish to find them. Legering sweetcorn or luncheon meat poses no problems, though.

Rod rests

The main requirement when legering is for the rod to be held as still as possible and for the line to run from reel to rod tip without being trapped at any point. The typical wide, float-rod rest-head is not ideal if there's any amount of wind as the rubber supports allow it to sway. You need one-piece plastic heads or some that are very stable indeed. And ideally you should have three, to give as much support as possible in very windy weather.

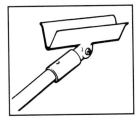

This type of rod rest helps to keep the rod steady in a wind.

The type I prefer to use near the head of the rod is about 3 in long; in other words 3 in of the rod. It has a deep V, which allows the line to run underneath the rod, and a swivel head so that you can adjust the angle to get it dead right. It must be on a very stout bank stick that is adjustable so the rod can be altered to cope with changing wind conditions or changing water level. Get a thick telescopic rest for this one – and one with a thumb screw as opposed to a collar, as the thumbscrew is more easily adjusted if the stick is well out from the bank.

Although some experienced anglers rest the butt of the rod on their knee or on their basket, this is not really ideal for the beginner, as there will always be some movement. You should aim to rest it on a rest most of the time. You can always transfer it to your knee if things are going well and you can see your bites easily. The butt should be within easy reach of your striking hand, and the new type of metal platform with swivelling arms or holders for bank sticks allows rod rests to be positioned well, even if the ground is rocky. This back one should also be adjustable as you may want to make several minor changes of position, bringing the rod tip closer to, or farther away from, the surface in the course of a day's fishing.

27

In a wind it's useful to use three rod rests to keep the rod steady.

With some rods you will see a noticeable sag in the middle when you have a rod rest at the butt and one near the head, and then you must have a third one to support the centre. The type is not as important as with the other two, but it must support the rod without trapping the line.

Too many anglers treat rod rests as an afterthought. However, for legering, when the rod may spend most of the time on its rests, it is crucial to get it into exactly the right position. It pays dividends in fewer missed bites. Whoever said that legering was the lazy man's way of fishing obviously never did it properly!

THE QUIVERTIP

Seeing a bite is probably the novice's biggest worry. In fact, it's no more difficult than seeing a bite on a float. And many people consider it easier because the rod is much closer than a float would be. Some anglers with failing eyesight leger for that very reason. The quivertip is certainly the most popular bite indicator now. And for the beginner it's probably the best choice. Not only is a quivertip slightly easier to cast than a swingtip, but it also tends to adjust itself more easily to the current or drift than a swingtip. It is, in fact, just a sensitive extension of the rod tip.

Some rods come equipped with several different top joints, each with its own built-in quivertip.

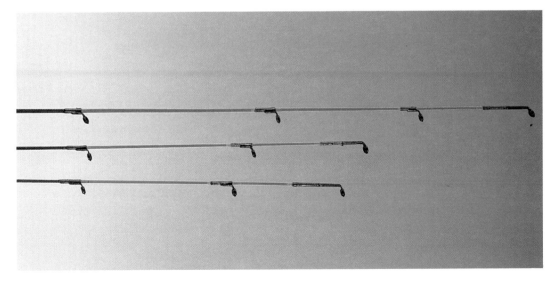

Built-in or screw-in?

You have two choices. Either you get a rod with a special, slim, sensitive, tip already built in as part of the rod, or you can buy a leger rod with a special threaded tip into which you can screw a quivertip of your choice. The screw-in type are on sale in most tackle shops and will range from very thin,

29

and hence very sensitive, to much thicker, and less sensitive. Broadly speaking, you should use the thin ones on windless days on stillwaters, and thicker ones on windy days on stillwaters or in running water, when a current would pull a thin tip right round.

Most experienced leger anglers have at least one favourite rod with its own quivertip built in. However, there's a type of rod that is becoming more and more popular – a leger rod with three or even four different top joints, each with a built-in quivertip. This will give a range of quivertips from very sensitive to very strong, and which between them will suit almost every occasion, except perhaps very fast rivers like the Severn when you will need a special, extra-strong swimfeeder rod.

Screw-in tips, however, can give the angler a huge range of tip strengths, colours and tapers, and in addition can be used with the same rod as a swingtip so you need only one leger rod. One disadvantage is that when a screw-in tip is screwed into the tip ring it's a matter of luck whether the rings on the tip line up with those on the rod. The answer is to slip a piece of stiff tubing over the quivertip thread – a piece of a ballpoint inner tube is ideal – which will allow you to align the rings easily and still get a good, solid fit.

For the beginner a rod with a threaded tip, allowing you to use a variety of tips at very little extra cost, is a good compromise. Later you will probably get at least one special quivertip rod suited to the waters you fish most.

Types of quivertip

This is largely a matter of personal choice, but on a stillwater the best sensitive tips tend to be long and tapered, and after a while you will be able to use such a tip in a great variety of conditions. On a perfectly still day such a tip will be straight out, and you will watch the very end for bites; on a windier day the end will bend round as the line is moved by the wind, and you will watch a point 1–2 in from the end to spot your bites. In both circumstances, you can see a bite developing very well and begin to visualise what the fish is doing with your bait, and when to strike. This is not as difficult as it sounds, particularly if you are able to sit in the open, without an umbrella up. You will be able to feel the gusts of wind as they blow round you, and get a better idea of the effect of the wind on the tip.

However, where you have a very sensitive, tapered tip you may find that when you are playing a fish the top few inches of the quivertip – perhaps most of it – doesn't come into play. This is no great problem so long as you realise what is happening, and don't slacken off when the tip starts to bend right round as a fish swims away.

Straight tips – those that have no taper at all – tend to be used on running waters, and help iron out the little bumps and quivers made by the current or by wisps of weed flowing down the river. In other words you get fewer false alarms. With a straight tip you are likely to be exerting pressure on the fish right from the top ring of the quivertip, which can be a help in giving you a little buffer if your rod is a bit stiff.

The material the tip is made from (it's nearly always fibreglass or carbon) is not particularly important. It's much more important that you can see it well and can 'read' it as a bite develops.

Long or short?

Long tips are normally used on deep, still waters as they take longer to straighten after you've cast, or tightened up, and make it easier to see bites 'on the drop' – that is, as the bait is sinking within, say 30, seconds of casting. You will find, when you start quivertipping, that a lot of your bites come just after you've cast in, or adjusted the tension on your line, or after you've moved the weight along the bottom. And a long tip gives you a much longer time to spot these bites – the process is more fully described in the chapter 'Tightening and Twitching'. With a short tip you may have to turn the reel every couple of seconds to tighten the line because the tip will spring back immediately. However, a short tip is very useful on medium-to-fast running water, on very windy days when a long tip would be blown all over the place, and on very shallow water, say up to no more than 3 ft deep. In these shallow stillwater swims a short tip can get you in touch with the tackle more quickly after you've cast than will a long tip.

Position of the rod

Most important of all is to get approximately a right-angle between your rod and the line. This will give the maximum

The angle between line and quivertip needs to be around 90°. If you're fishing in front of you the rod will need to be roughly parallel with the bank, as shown.

31

Left: the line should make approximately a right-angle with the rod. In windy weather drop the tip to the surface so the wind doesn't blow the line about.

Right: it's usual to sit with your back to the wind when legering. A target board like this helps you spot bites.

amount of movement of the tip for the least effort on the part of the fish. And nine times out of ten you will have your rod placed approximately parallel with the bank, but with the rod tip over the water, clear of bankside vegetation. If you're fishing directly in front of you, you will get away with the rod at anything up to 45° to the bank, but if it's more than that you're going to struggle to see bites unless they're real sail-aways.

On running water, unless the flow is very slight indeed, it's generally better to sit facing downstream. Then, when you make a strike, you are tending to strike with the current.

On a stillwater, it's usually better to sit with your back to the wind. Not only is this more comfortable, especially if it starts to rain, but you are helping to shield the butt end of your rod from the wind. And although you may not realise it, the effect of the wind on your rod butt is probably at least as important as that on the line and rod tip – every little movement of the butt makes the tip dance horribly. If the rod is set perfectly solidly, you'll be able to see proper bites much more easily. Check that next time you're fishing in a wind.

In a strong wind one way of minimising false bites is to tighten the line so it holds the tip under pressure. This is against all the rules, which say it's not necessary to tighten line completely, but it may be your best compromise in very difficult circumstances. Actually there is a better answer – a form of slack-lining – but more of that later.

The colour of the tip is optional, though most commercially made, screw-in quivertips seem to have 2 or 3 in of red on the end. Certainly the vast majority of anglers like a bright colour here. White is also a good colour, and many anglers carry a bottle of typist's correction fluid to colour the tip quickly.

A method of spotting difficult bites

Most anglers will be looking for the quivertip to bend obviously when they get a bite, and indeed the quivertip is capable of showing minute movements. However, there is a useful method of seeing the tiniest of bites. If you sit directly behind the rod so it looks straight, or as straight as you can make it, you can move your head so that the side of the tip ring just peeks out from the side of the rod. Settle in that position, and when the tip ring is pulled round by even the tiniest fraction of an inch, you will see it. It's a method for those days in winter when small fish are hanging on to the bait without giving any obvious indication – the silver of the tip ring will make it very easy to see.

Safely in the net at last. This carp fell to quivertipped red maggots.

33

Target boards

Target boards are extremely popular with leger anglers and most useful with a quivertip. They are usually black and rectangular and screw into a bank stick. They have lines or a grid marked on them, and are placed beyond the end of the rod, so the angler can line up his tip ring with one of the lines. Once the tip is set into position it is easy to see it move even a fraction of an inch.

In addition, when there is floating weed about, the board can be set so it diverts the weed round the tip so that it does not catch on the line, provided you are sitting with the board upstream of the rod tip. And it can also keep wind off the tip. If you are caught out without a target board, a bank stick pushed into the bottom just beyond the rod tip is a useful substitute.

Position of the rod tip

You will find, nine times out of ten, that the best position for your tip ring on a stillwater is just above the surface – perhaps no more than a ¼ in – with the rest of the line beneath the water. This position stops the wind buffetting the line. It also helps you spot some of the tiny bites you might otherwise miss, as your eye will quickly become accustomed to judging the gap between water surface and tip ring. If the gap is a ¼ in, then a movement of your tip of only a ¼ in will reduce the gap by anything up to 50 per cent (given that the line is at an angle) – and the human brain is incredibly adept at spotting this. However, if there is marginal weed you may have to lift the rod high, and perhaps even have it set pointing towards the sky. Then you can do nothing about the effect of the wind on the line – like all types of fishing, legering is always a compromise between what you would like to do and what the elements and circumstances allow. If you can get that rod point low, then do so.

Types of bite

Experience will enable you to decide what is a bite and what isn't and – just as important – when it's worth striking at a bite. Most often, the sort of bite that pulls the tip round by about 1 in and then immediately lets it flick back to its original position is unhittable. And after a few outings you will start to learn that this sort of indication is simply not worth striking at.

Often this is a line bite, caused by a small fish flicking the line somewhere between your rod tip and the leger weight. If it's not that, it's likely to be a very small fish that has nipped the end of your maggot and given it a quick tweak. Line bites caused by bigger fish tend to pull round fast, but usually pull round further and hold the position for perhaps half a second before flicking back into place. Unfortunately, these bites often give you sufficient time to make an instinctive strike before you realise it's a false alarm.

If you are missing bites, and suspect line bites, the best thing is to sit on your hands – literally – so you can't make a premature strike, for continual striking and re-casting into a shoal of fish that hasn't settled down to feed can eventually unsettle them so much that they move away. Better to allow too long than to strike too quickly. In other words, it's better to let a fish get away with your bait than to risk either pricking it in the lip and losing it or scaring it by striking when the line is lying across, or perhaps round or underneath, its body.

A proper bite, contrary to what many anglers may imagine, is often no more than a tiny, slow, nudge – the sort you will never see unless you are concentrating really hard. This is frequently from a fish that is slowly cruising around the bottom and picks up your bait confidently, never imagining there might a hook in it. It has no reason to bolt away; it just carries on cruising around, perhaps moving only 1–2 in at a time. When you get a series of these tiny, little nudges you almost always connect with every one, as opposed to the real sail-aways, when the quivertip may hurtle round and keep on going, half of which you miss!

Striking on a hunch

Don't worry to begin with about whether you're able to spot all your bites – you most certainly won't. Once you're comfortable with your tackle don't be afraid to strike on a 'hunch'. All experienced quivertip anglers suddenly find themselves striking without being really sure whether they've had a bite or not. It's almost as if the human brain can programme itself to recognise a strange movement of the tip and give the orders to strike before you realise it is happening.

The more relaxed you are, provided you're really concentrating on the tip, the more likely you are to get the feeling – no more than that – that there's a fish at the bait. Sometimes the tip doesn't bend round – it just 'quivers', hence the name quivertip.

35

CHAPTER THREE

THE SWINGTIP

A swingtip, as its name implies, swings about on the end of the rod, and lifts when you get a bite. It's most useful on deep stillwaters, but can be used effectively on all waters, including rivers where the water is moving. However, it's usual on really fast rivers to discard the swingtip in favour of either a strong quivertip, or a special swimfeeder rod, when you watch the rod tip for bites.

As with a quivertip, it's possible to buy a rod with a swingtip already whipped on to the end. For most anglers there is little point in buying one of these, because there is a huge range of swingtips, which will all screw into the same threaded end ring as any quivertip.

On quivertips the ring spacings at the rod tip are not particularly important. However, there is one point you should watch when buying, or making up, a swingtip. You must have a ring near the threaded end. If you don't (and

Swingtips come in different models and sizes. From the top: the Clayton one-piece nylon swingtip; extra-heavy metal; heavy cane with three rings; stiff link for strong wind; flourescent-tipped for night fishing.

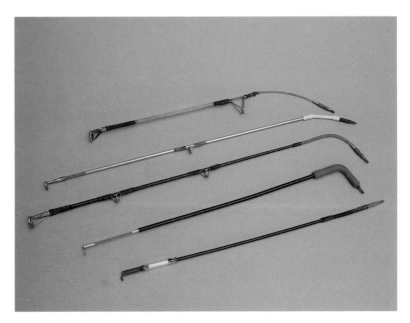

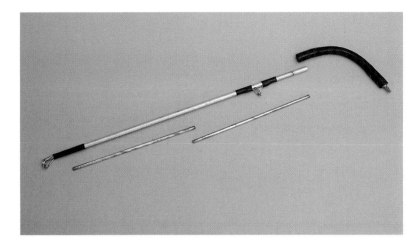

Left: The take-apart model has weights which are inserted down the hollow swingtip, so you can adjust its weight. The swingtip pushes into the rubber link.

Below: Waiting for a bite! Note the special long rod rest near the tip.

many swingtips are sold with no ring here) you will find that the line can flick over the tip of your rod, causing a break when you strike.

The swingtip can be left hanging vertically downwards after you have cast, but, at least to begin with, you will probably feel more confident allowing it to hang at a slight angle, under very light tension. You should be certain of seeing an indication when a fish takes the bait.

37

It's easier to see bites on the drop with a long tip, though it's more prone to the effects of wind.

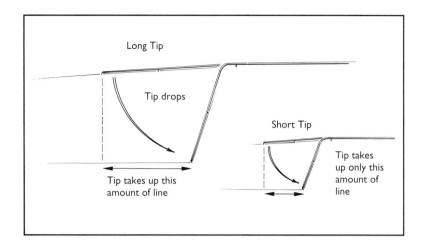

Weight and length

There's no taper to worry about with swingtips, like there is with a quivertip – all swingtips are straight. Your choice will be concerned with weight and length. Obviously a heavier one will tend to swing about less in a wind and will not be pulled up so far by a heavy drift or in running water. This means that it will be easier to see bites, as the tip will have a greater distance to travel before it's pulled out perfectly straight. That's a broad generalisation, but to begin with you should aim at using a light swingtip on stillwaters when there's not too much wind, and heavier swingtips on moving water or in really bad conditions on stillwaters. As for the length, a short one will swing around less in a wind, while there may be some circumstances in which it is essential to get your rod as close as possible to the water – bankside or wind conditions may dictate this. In that case a short swingtip will be needed.

However, in reasonable conditions on slow or still waters the average-length swingtip – about 10 in – will be a good choice. This gives you enough time to spot bites 'on the drop' combined with a reasonable amount of stability in a wind.

Some anglers fish with swingtips almost 2 ft long. Each time they are tightened, they take up more slack line than a shorter one, and this is an advantage when bites occur as the bait falls ('on the drop'), or soon after the bait has settled. Also, the longer the swingtip, the easier it is to see bites – a 1-in pull on a short tip may be hardly noticeable, but on a very long tip it's more obvious because there is more swingtip moving! However, you are better off using a normal-length swingtip until you have completely mastered the basics. Taking up slack line in such a way that it helps you see bites is a much misunderstood part of legering, and the swingtip offers the best way of doing this.

The Clayton type

If there is an 'all-round' swingtip it must be the original Clayton-type marketed by the late Jack Clayton, a Boston, Lincs, tackle dealer who popularised the swingtip in the 1950s. This is a one-piece swingtip made of extruded nylon. The link is pliable, but with enough stiffness to hold the tip under just a little pressure against the wind. It's a light tip, and not easy to find nowadays. If you can find any, especially the medium-to-long ones from 10–18 in in length, buy some. They'll come in handy in the future.

Plastic types

In any typical tackle shop there will be many modern swingtips, probably made from some sort of plastic. Look for weight, length and the type of link. It's advisable to have a reasonable selection to begin with, though later you will probably end up with just two or three favourites. Perhaps the most important thing about the 'average' commercial swingtip is the link. On a stillwater it really is useful to have a link that has a little stiffness in it, enabling you to increase its resistance to the wind by turning the rod slightly.

Heavy cane

There are also heavy cane types, most useful on medium-moving water. They'll probably have a simple pliable rubber link, which makes them liable to be blown all over the place in wind. That doesn't matter so much on moving water, when the current puts the line and the swingtip under tension, tightening the line and reducing the effect of the wind.

Take-apart

The take-apart swingtip is an extremely handy and greatly underrated item of tackle. It consists of a standard, threaded end, onto which is pushed a piece of rubber tubing. Into the tubing is pushed a hollow swingtip, and it comes with a set of metal weights that are slipped down inside the swingtip. This enables you to adjust the weight more quickly than with any other method, and is faster than using lead wire.

The removeable swingtip

Removeable swingtips, which can be clipped on or removed without breaking down the tackle, have gone out of fashion. However, it's possible to adapt the ones you already have. To

Lead wire wrapped round a swingtip to steady it in a wind.

do this, take off the tip ring and substitute a large necklace clip. This enables you to clip it over the line at any time. Araldite the tip ring into place, adding a second ring near the threaded end if possible. Just remember to screw the swingtip into the threaded end ring before you clip the line into the clips.

Great sport at dusk

If you're going to fish until it's dark, the swingtip has a huge advantage over the quivertip, and will allow you at least 30 minutes extra fishing time. You can see a swingtip move far more easily than you'll ever see a quivertip pull round, especially if you can position it over the water so it's silhouetted against the reflection of the sky. This applies even if the quivertip has reflective paint on it – don't forget that reflective paint only works if it's got light to reflect!

You can also get swingtips with a luminous end, and these are extremely useful as dusk falls. You must remember, though, to expose them to light during the day otherwise they won't work very well. If you think you might need it, take one out earlier in the day and leave it on your tackle box. Or you can clip a luminous Starlite on the end. This is a modern chemical miracle – you bend the tube, which is about 1 in long, and the chemical reaction gives off light for several hours. You can fish with this tucked into the bank, rather than having to silhouette it against the sky. You won't be able to see much of the tip, but you'll see the gleaming, disembodied end rise perfectly when you get a bite. And of course bites from dusk onwards tend to be bolder than those in the day, as the fish gain confidence under cover of darkness.

Lead wire

One of the most useful bits of equipment for a swingtipper is a length of lead wire, which you can buy in tackle shops. Wind it neatly round the end of a light swingtip to adjust its weight. Not only can you get the tip to set exactly at the right angle, but you can also adjust it by adding or subtracting wire as the wind alters or as a current picks up or dies away. The Clayton type of swingtip is ideally suited to this treatment.

Lead wire is used a lot on the Fen drains, which are exposed to wind and have high banks that tend to funnel the wind, often creating conditions similar to those at sea – big waves with white crests. Then you need something to steady the swingtip.

A heavy wind can also set up big drifts that are almost as fierce as a medium-paced river. A light swingtip will be pulled up straight in these conditions, so you need to add weight to

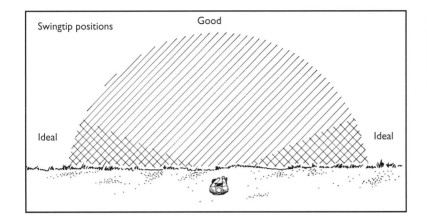

A swingtip can be placed in any position, though most anglers find it easier to see bites if it is placed to the side.

Fenland bream expert Syd Meads favours long swingtips for seeing bites on the drop.

41

hold it down. And although classed as stillwaters all the Fen drains, like the Somerset drains, are prone to be pumped at a moment's notice and at all sorts of times. This can happen after heavy rains, or even when heavy rain is forecast. Other drains don't have pumps, but are controlled by sluice gates, which are lifted when the tidal rivers are low. So a water that has been completely still may run for, say, an hour, then stop. Then there may be a short period of still water followed by a movement back upstream; followed, finally, by still water again.

No single swingtip will be ideal for all those situations, and the addition or removal of lead wire is the best alternative to changing the swingtip, which would normally mean completely breaking down the tackle and re-ringing the swingtip before re-tying the leger bomb and hook.

Position of the rod

The swingtip is much more versatile than the quivertip when it comes to positioning your rod. Whereas with a quivertip you aim to get approximately a right-angle between the rod and the line, with a swingtip this angle is of no real importance. This is because the link will allow the swingtip to be pulled upwards in any direction. So you can place the rod anywhere in the 180° arc in front of you: pointing to the left, parallel with the bank, or straight out, or round to the right, or at any spot in between. However, for the sake of comfort the average angler will instinctively sit with his back to the wind, and this helps shield the rod from the wind. The swingtip can also be shielded by tucking the rod into the bankside vegetation. The only proviso is that the rod will need to be approximately parallel with the surface of the water.

In moving water most anglers will tend to try to sit with the rod facing downstream. Then when they strike they are doing so across the flow rather than against it, assuming they are fishing a spot somewhere out in front of them. There are times when the wind and the water are coming from opposite

Putting the end of the swingtip just under the surface is an excellent way of beating the problems caused by floating rubbish.

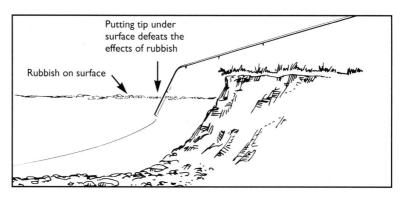

Putting tip under surface defeats the effects of rubbish

Rubbish on surface

directions, of course, and that's when only you can decide on your priorities. The position, though, makes a big difference to the way you see your bites. With the rod straight out in front of you, you are watching the tip move directly away from you, and it can be difficult to spot bites in wind. However, if the rod is parallel to the bank, you are watching the swingtip move across your line of sight when you get a bite, and most anglers find these sorts of bites very much easier to spot. There's also a difference with the striking. With the rod resting to the side, a strike pulls the line roughly along its own length, or through its own 'tube' as it was once described, and this means the line meets very little resistance. With the rod put straight out in front of you, however, a strike is, in effect, pulling the line upwards through the water.

In theory, the sideways strike means that you are striking directly to the fish, while the upwards strike means that the line is meeting lots of resistance and the strike is not direct. However, some of the top bream anglers prefer pointing the rod straight out in front of them if conditions allow, so the final choice is up to you. Where bream are concerned, most anglers strike too early anyway, so it can be worth trying the straight-out approach if you are missing bites, as this may slow your strike fractionally.

On most occasions you will want to position the rod so that the very end of the swingtip just touches, or is just above, the surface. On a really calm day when there's just a tiny drift on a stillwater you can, with a little patience, allow the drift to take the line up so that the tip is just held down by the surface tension of the water. That's the perfect scenario – the tiniest of bites will flick the tip above the surface in a way you can't possibly miss.

On a windy day it can actually pay to allow ½ in of the swingtip to remain in the water as this has a steadying effect. It helps if the bottom inch or so is brightly coloured, in which case you watch the top edge of the coloured band for bites, and not the very tip. The colour is a matter of personal preference. Some of the modern glowing colours have been known to cause migraines. A black swingtip with a white tip or white bands can be effective. My preference in good light is for a black swingtip with a single white band about 1 in from the end. When I sink the tip I drop this band to surface level and watch it for bites.

When you have gained experience in legering you may find that you can see bites in a good light no matter what the colour of the indicator you are using. However, undoubtedly there are times, during poor light conditions, when you will be glad of a bright colour on the end of your swingtip. As with floatfishing, a pair of polaroid spectacles can help reduce eyestrain when you're looking at a tip for hours on end.

The ideal setting for a swingtip – just touching the surface.

Bites

A swingtip is, generally, more affected by wind than is a quivertip. A swingtip is fatter, while a quivertip is very thin; and even under some tension a swingtip is liable to be blown in almost any direction, while a quivertip's movement is much more restricted. This is the price you pay for being able to use a swingtip in almost any position. However, to begin with you may find a swingtip harder to read.

The ideal bite is a slow lift, with the swingtip ending straight out, almost parallel with the water. You should rarely miss a bite like this. The difficult bite is the one that lifts the indicator perhaps ½ in and then allows it to drop back, and this can happen before you realise you have a bite, especially

44

in a wind. On a quivertip this would register as quite a good pull, and you would probably strike. In fact, it rarely hurts to leave a bite like this and wait for a better indication, and you are more likely to find yourself doing this if you use a swingtip. The end result is that most swingtippers tend to hit a greater proportion of bites they strike at than quivertippers.

If you get that tiny lift and nothing else, it's worth striking the next time you get one, even if the tip has fallen right back. And you are likely to hit a higher proportion of bites by striking late using a swingtip than when using a quivertip. I can't work out why this is. It may be something to do with the fact that the tension on a quivertip increases noticeably as it bends, while the power needed to pull a swingtip up varies very little during the lift, and the fish feels more confident, and keeps the bait in its mouth. Also, the amount of line that can be pulled by the fish is greater with a swingtip than with a quivertip. A 12-in swingtip hanging vertically won't be out straight until more than 12 in of line have been pulled, while a 12-in pull on a quivertip will probably pull the rod off the rest

There are times, though, when little fish do seem put off by the weight of the swingtip, and keep jerking it without ever making off with the bait. A change to a quivertip, which is lighter, is then probably the answer.

Line bites, caused by fish hitting the line between bait and rod tip, are likely to be more easily recognised on a swingtip than on any other method. The tip will, without warning, shoot out and immediately fall back, probably leaving some extra slack line – this slack line can be the result of the fish moving the leger weight. And you are less likely to hit a bite like this instinctively on a swingtip than with a quivertip, which is a point in favour of the swingtip, especially when fishing for bream.

Swingtip or quivertip?

If you are uncertain which method to use, here are some useful rules of thumb:
  • If the water is quite fast use a quivertip.
  • If you have to point your rod straight out in front of you because of bankside vegetation, go for a swingtip.
  • If you're expecting tentative bites use a quivertip.
  • If you're expecting good sail-away bites use a swingtip as this allows you to see the bite developing.
  • If there's a very strong side wind use a quivertip because it's easier to sink the line immediately after casting and it's likely to be less affected by the wind.
  • If the light is very bad, a swingtip will be easier to see.
  • If you're expecting bites on the drop, choose a swingtip.

45

CHAPTER FOUR

BUTT INDICATORS

A butt indicator is clipped on to the rod, usually somewhere on the butt joint, with the arm hanging down. The line is threaded through the end of the arm, the cast made, the rod pointed down towards the water, usually with the end actually under water, and a little slack line is let out so that the arm hangs at around 45°. When you get a bite the line tightens and the arm swings upwards. Or, more rarely, you may get a slack-line bite, when the arm will drop down to a near-vertical position. The great advantage of this type of indicator, when it is fixed to the butt, is that it is extremely close to the angler, so it can be seen easily. Also, it is easy to shield the arm from the wind, as it can be tucked nicely inside an umbrella right beside the angler.

The arm is normally between 5–8 in long, but the length is relatively unimportant so long as you can see it move upwards when you get a bite. As for colour, this is less important than it is for a swingtip or quivertip, both of which are often viewed against a background of water, where ripple can make bites difficult to see. But the butt indicator will usually be seen against the bankside vegetation at a very short distance. However, for the angler fishing at night a piece of reflective or luminous tape is essential, or some sort of arrangement which will allow a chemical night light to be attached to the arm.

Types of butt indicator

The swinging arms have either a floppy joint of rubber tubing or a type of tiny metal hinge. The latter type allows the arm to move directly upwards or down, and not to one side, while the floppy connection allows the arm to swing around in all directions. Nevertheless, the tube type does not corrode or stick, and is generally to be preferred to the metal hinges, which can easily stick. When you reel in, the indicator will tap against the rod, but will not foul the line in any way.

One very useful variation has either a split ring on the end, so that the indicator can be fixed or removed at will without breaking down the tackle, or a necklace-type ring which can be opened to release or insert the line. It is not necessary even to have a complete ring. Some indicators have a half-moon shaped wire, which merely lies on the line. Then, when you reel in the arm comes off the line and hangs harmlessly out of the way.

Position of the indicator

The butt indicator will always have a spring clip, which allows it to be pushed on to the butt. The earliest models were pushed on under the butt joint, with the arm swinging below. However, some more modern types are pushed on to the side of the butt, still with the arm swinging up and down, but by the side of the rod. Others have a smaller spring clip, which allows them to be clipped on to any joint, even the rod tip, though there are few advantages in having the indicator this high up the rod, since it will usually be more difficult to see and less stable in a wind. The arm in this case is usually shorter because the space between the rings is smaller. All work on the same principle of the arm moving up towards the horizontal position as the line tightens. The position of the indicator on the rod is a matter of preference – the most important point is that it should be easily visible.

To get the best out of the indicator it should be positioned on the rod so that the single tip ring through which the line runs is exactly half-way between two rod rings when the line is tight. This gives it the greatest amount of movement for any given pull on the line. Where the clip goes is immaterial – so long as the end ring is correctly positioned. It's usual to have the clip positioned so the arm is pointing towards the tip, but even that is not a hard and fast rule. It will still work if it points towards the angler.

Position of the rod

This is very important. For while with a swingtip or quivertip there is nothing to obstruct the line between fish and indicator when you get a bite, with a butt indicator the line has to run most of the length of the rod before the indicator moves. And though theoretically there is friction between the line and the rod rings the really big problems occur at the rod's tip ring. If you place the rod parallel with the bank, as with a quivertip, with the line making a right-angle to the rod, the fish has to pull the line 'round the corner' before moving the indicator, and this creates friction. So the correct position must be with the rod allowing the line to run straight through the tip ring and down the rod with no obstruction.

47

A modern-style butt indicator in position. This one has a flexible rubber link, and the tip just lays on the line.

Many textbooks tell you to point the rod at the bait. This is good basic advice, but in fact you should point the rod at the point where the line enters the water, which may be some way to one side of you if your bait is straight out in front and there is a bow in the line caused by current or a strong drift. This position reduces the friction between line and the tip ring of the rod to a minimum. If you don't pay attention to this point, and allow an angle to develop at the rod tip, the fish will feel resistance before you see a bite on the indicator, and may drop the bait.

The ideal rod for use with a butt indicator is similar to that needed for slack lining (see Chapter 5). It should be reasonably stiff, so that the tip doesn't blow about in a high wind. A butt indicator can, of course, be used with any quivertip rod, but the tiny rings on a quivertip aren't ideal, as

When using a butt indicator always point the rod straight down the line, not directly at the bait.

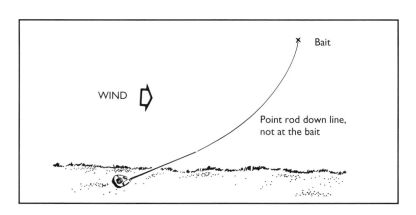

Bait

WIND

Point rod down line, not at the bait

they don't allow the line enough room to run freely. Also, a sensitive quivertip is liable to waggle from side to side in a wind, increasing the chance of resistance and certainly giving false bite indications.

The rod tip should normally be placed 1 in or so under the surface if possible. In really windy conditions it may be necessary to place it deeper so the wind does not blow directly on the line between rod tip and water. However, the deeper you place it, the more resistance you will have on the strike, so you will always have to compromise. The best advice is to concentrate first on getting bites and making sure you can see them, and worry about striking later. There is

In very difficult conditions a butt indicator, being less sensitive than a quivertip, will often catch fish.

49

another reason for putting the rod tip under the surface. It helps steady the rod in a wind. This is the same principle as putting the end of a swingtip under water to stop it swinging about.

Floating weed

The butt indicator is perhaps the best method of all for beating the menace of floating weed, whether on stillwater or a river. For the rod tip can be pushed under the surface as far as you wish – it makes no difference to the bite indication. The first 2 in of water holds 99 per cent of floating rubbish, so 4 in under is usually the maximum you will need to sink the tip. There's still the possibility of the line itself catching weed, of course. There's no way of getting out of that one – you simply have to get the point at which the rod enters the water as close to the bankside as possible to minimise the problem. This may just entail sitting back from the water's edge, pointing the rod down as much as you dare, and tucking the tip behind some sort of cover. As with all methods of legering on rivers, canals or drains where the wind blows weed along, a target board can help if it's pushed in just upstream of the rod tip, with its base well under the surface so that it deflects weed around it.

Setting the indicator

This is easier than with the swingtip or quivertip, though it's not as good at picking out bites on the drop. You will need to cast out and watch the line between the rod tip and the surface to tell when the leger weight has hit the bottom. As the weight is falling the line shoots out, and when it has hit the bottom the line slows. It doesn't always stop dead. At this point click over the bale arm, tighten until you think you have some sort of contact with the leger weight, and put the rod in the correct position, with no angle between rod tip and line.

All you can do now is to tighten until the arm is under full tension and pointing straight down the rod, then let some line out from the reel until the arm is hanging roughly 45° downwards. When you've had some experience with the butt indicator you can take your time about tightening up, and may spot bites as you do so, but it's not as easy as with either a swingtip or the quivertip, as the arm tends to move in jerks rather than smoothly, and it's difficult to interpret these movements. It may be because the arm is closer to you, but bites seem to take you more by surprise with a butt indicator than with a swingtip or quivertip.

On running water you may need to add lead wire to hold the arm down, in the same way as recommended for the swingtip. A really experienced swingtipper may be able to fish with his tip almost straight out in a current, with no wire added. However, this is not possible with an indicator, as once it's pointing straight down the rod no further movement is possible. And in fast water you will find the indicator becomes very difficult to use anyway. A switch to a strong quivertip is then called for.

The indicator comes into its own on stillwaters, which may have rollers on them caused by wind. And in these conditions you may find that each time a wave slams against the rod the indicator jerks. You'll soon get used to this movement, though to begin with you may be tempted to strike. Just dip the rod point down as far as you dare under the surface.

Bites

The ideal bite is a slow movement upwards, causing the indicator to go out perfectly straight. This is a typical bream bite, and you can be in no doubt about what it is. However, for roach and other species the indicator often does little more than jerk upwards and stay there, perhaps falling slowly back to its original position. It is much less versatile than a swingtip, and has a much smaller distance to travel during the course of a bite. For this reason you will find that a long arm is preferable to a short one most of the time. It enables you to read the bite better as it takes longer to straighten. Also you will find that it usually pays to fish with an arm that is on the heavy side, as it falls back more readily when you get a slack-line bite.

All round the butt indicator is less sensitive than most other legering indicators, but for that very reason it is useful in difficult conditions. If you habitually strike too soon using other methods, or miss a lot of bites, you may find that a butt indicator increases your catch rate, because it won't show as many false bites caused by rubbish or wind hitting the line. And because it is positioned closer to the angler than any other form of bite indication, it gives many people extra confidence. If you want to try an indicator, the best time to do it is when you're getting lots of bites on a quivertip. Add a butt indicator, adjust the position of the rod and give it a go. A quivertip is not ideal if conditions are really rough, but at least you'll see how a butt indicator behaves when you get a bite.

Striking

Because the rod points down the line it will almost always be pointing somewhere out in front of you, and you will have to strike upwards and over your shoulder. This is not ideal, as there is resistance from the water because you are pulling the

51

line up against it, rather than through it – the same problem as that encountered by the swingtip angler who has his rod pointing forwards. It works, however, possibly because there tends to be less slack between rod and fish than with any other legering method. It does mean, nevertheless, that a rod with an all-through action is best, as it will absorb any possible overstrike. A stiff rod with spliced tip may lead to breaks if you strike too hard.

Above: Problems with weed? A butt indicator is usually one of the best solutions, although here the weed close in would need to be moved first.

Right: A Fenland bream goes into the net. Butt indicators are still used here by locals, to beat the wind.

CHAPTER FIVE

SLACK-LINING AND OTHER METHODS

The art of slacklining has been slowly lost since the advent of the quivertip and swingtip. However, if conditions allow its use it can be the most deadly method of legering. No indicator is added. The angler watches the line for bites, usually the section of line between the rod tip and the water.

A nice steady wind, and the bream are feeding – perfect conditions for slacklining.

This acts like an extremely light swingtip, lifting when a fish makes off with the bait.

The conditions must be right, however. There must be no movement on the water at all, or if there is movement, the wind must be against the flow or drift, and hard enough to form a bow in the line. A strong flow will cause the line to drag round and tighten, leaving no slack line for a fish to move when it takes the bait. In those conditions slacklining is out of the question, and if you tried it you would, effectively, be watching your rod tip for bites – in which case a quivertip is the answer.

Slacklining has the advantage over swingtips and quivertips that, generally, the stronger the wind the better the method will work, provided the water is not moving. And it is possible to catch fish in conditions so bad that all other methods are futile. The rod should be stiff, if possible. As with the butt indicator it is possible to use any rod, but a quivertip will wash around in the wind, causing the line to jerk and giving false bites to the inexperienced slackliner, while a floppy rod will bounce around on the rests, causing the same problems.

There was a glassfibre, two-piece rod made once, named the Fenman, with the tip ring 1 in back from the rod tip. A swingtip could be pushed onto the end of the tip using just a piece of rubber tubing. It was a thick, stiff, 8-ft rod that would be laughed at now, when compared with a modern, sleek, carbon tip-action legering rod. However, short and stiff, with an all-through action, it could be wedged into position in the strongest wind, hardly moving and allowing perfect bite registration for the slackliner.

Position of the rod

Usually the most comfortable position is almost parallel with the bank, with your back to the wind, and with the rod about 6 in from the surface. However, you can fish it in any position so long as you can see the point at which the line enters the water, and you will usually find it easier to see the line if the sun is not directly behind you. The line shows up better if the light strikes it at an angle, as it looks whiter. You will have to juggle round with positions to find the best one.

Letting out the slack

This is perhaps easier than for any other legering method. And in fact in a strong wind it is often only necessary to cast out, ensure the line is sunk, and then put the rod on the rest and allow the wind to take up all the slack line, for the bigger the bow, the better you will see the bite. However, for your first attempts it is advisable to cast, tighten down to the bomb, and then let out a given amount of line. Knowing that you have, say, just 3 or 4 in of slack line bowing in the wind will give you confidence that you will see a bite when you get one.

It is much easier to see a normal pull-away bite than you might imagine. Given a good bite, the bow of line will pull straight, and you can be in no doubt that a fish is at the bait. Bream will usually give a bite like this, even though on a quivertip or swingtip the bite appears hesitant. A bite from, say, a small roach, which might appear as a tiny tap on a quivertip rod, is seen as a sudden straightening of the bow followed by an immediate fall back. In a gusty wind this can be difficult to spot, but in a steady wind, no matter how hard, it's not difficult.

The bait is usually twitched by leaving the rod on the rest and pulling the line between the reel and the butt ring, which will cause the bow to straighten. Then keep pulling until a bow forms again. If there's a bit of a wind you can then let go of all the slack line, and the result will be a bigger bow – but you'll still see the bites. In a very light wind that doesn't immediately take up all the slack, you wind in until the bow re-forms to your liking.

Windless days

On those occasions when there is no wind, some anglers use a very interesting method. They cast out and allow the bomb to settle while holding the rod in the air. Then they lay the rod on the rest without tightening at all, and allow the line to float on the surface. Bites are shown either as a distinct twitching of the line at the point where it disappears below the surface, or it will rapidly start to pull down into the water.

Extra-windy days

On those days when the wind is so rough that bite detection, even with a strong quivertip, appears impossible, you can see bites by pointing the rod roughly down the line, dipping the rod tip well under the surface, and pulling plenty of slack line out. Then allow a series of bows to develop between each ring on the rod – this may entail actually putting the rod in a fairly exposed position so it catches as much wind as possible. A bite is quite amazing – the series of bows suddenly disappears as the line is pulled tight. On these sorts of days fish are often feeding avidly and giving good bites anyway, so you should have no difficulty at all in seeing a bite.

55

Methods of slacklining: left, for normal slacklining watch the line just beyond the rod tip; right, in a high wind give extra slack line and allow the wind to blow loops of line from between the rings; when you get a bite they will all straighten at once. It may work even better if you put the rod tip under the surface.

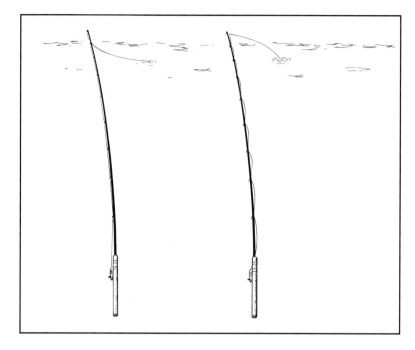

Lines

A light-coloured line is usually easiest to see, as it reflects light better and enables you to pick out the bow. But the best lines of all for slacklining used to be White Spider and Black Spider. These were braided terylene, I think, and were pure white and jet black, but I have not seen them on sale for many years now. However, both stood out in all conditions far better than any nylon line.

The bobbin

These were originally known as 'dough bobbins' because a piece of paste was placed on the line between the reel and butt ring and the line allowed to hang slack. The line straightens when you get a bite and the paste will eventually fall off when you play a fish. In fact, anything can be placed against the line at this spot – silver paper, a special little round ball that hooks over the line, or even just a stick laid against, or on, the line. A stick has the advantage of being left on the ground when a fish straightens the line, so at least you know you have had a bite even if you missed seeing it.

One variation is to wind a rubber-band around the top end of the rod handle, and tuck a loop of line into it. When you get a bite, the line pulls free and, again, you can see when you've had a bite. Another very popular idea is to use the top of a Fairy Liquid bottle. This can be clipped on the line just

56

above the butt ring. It's bright red, and you reel in with it still in position, take it off to cast, and then re-clip it in place.

Monkey climbers

These are a variation on the butt indicator. They are used on stillwaters, usually by anglers after big fish. The line is threaded through a ring that is placed on a vertical steel rod pushed into the bank. Slack line is pulled from the reel after the line has been tightened to the bait, and the ring allowed to slide up and down the metal rod, which is usually marked in segments. When a fish takes the bait the ring rises as the line tightens.

The great advantages of this sort of indicator, though it looks crude when compared with a swingtip, are that it is positioned near the angler, is big enough to see from a distance, and can be easily lit at night. And if you miss seeing a bite, you'll know you've had one because the ring will have been pulled off the end of the metal rod and will be swinging free.

Monkey climbers are a sophisticated form of bobbin.

Electronic bite alarms

The first audible alarm ever described in angling books must have been the system whereby a pebble was placed on a small piece of cardboard over the line, and balanced on the edge of a hollow tin. When the line straightened, it lifted the cardboard and the pebble fell off into the tin. Things are a bit more sophisticated – and more reliable – now, thanks to battery-operated bite alarms that not only give off a buzzing noise (this can be adjusted on the more sophisticated models

Electronic alarms are very popular with specimen hunters, particularly those who fish at night.

57

so that you can have two different sounds for two different rods), but which may also have a light so that at night you can see which one is sounding. Models range from those that give a straight buzz to others that can tell you how fast the line is peeling off the reel – also very useful at night. Prices vary accordingly, with the better ones being quite expensive but good value for money if you do a lot of night fishing.

Daytime anglers sometimes use bite alarms if they are using more than one rod. You must check, however, that more than one rod is allowed on the water, and check what the maximum number is. Also remember that to leave a rod unattended is against National Rivers Authority (NRA) by-laws, and you can be prosecuted for doing this. NRA by-laws also limit the number of rods that can be used by an angler at any one time.

Float legering

This is a very under-used method of legering, giving one important advantage over any other method – a float helps keep line out of bottom-growing weed that would otherwise foul the line. And on banks fringed with lillies it will keep the line between angler and float either right on the surface or just under it, stopping it from descending into the weeds and getting snagged. There are several methods of attaching the float, all involving a bottom-only fixing, and all normally used on still or very slowly moving water. If you want to float-leger on faster waters it would still, in theory, be possible using a float fixed top and bottom.

The good news is that you don't have to set the depth exactly right. In 6 ft of water you can have the float 7 ft from the leger weight, and still get perfect bites by tightening the line and pulling the float towards you until it cocks.

Float legering with a stop on the line (top) enables you to beat bankside weed. You can float leger without any stop (bottom) provided you can get your rod tip below the base of the float, which naturally rises to its highest point.

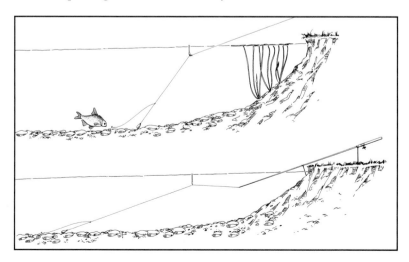

Fixed floats

This involves fixing an antenna float (now frequently, and incorrectly, called a waggler) on the line in the normal way. You are limited to the depth at which you can easily cast such a rig because of the heavy leger weight on the end of the line, which makes the rig more difficult to cast than a normal float set-up. As a general rule, you will run into trouble when the difference between the depth and the length of the rod is less than about 3 ft, and even then you will probably have to stand to cast out. So with a 10-ft rod a distance of about 7 ft between float and weight is the maximum you can easily cast. The rod tip is placed just under the surface and the line is tensioned until the float cocks correctly. To lower the float, reel in a little; to let more of it show, let some line out.

Sliding float

A much better bet than the fixed float, on most waters, is a sliding float, with a line stop placed at the correct position on the line. The float will slide back up the line after you've cast, until it meets the stop. Then you tighten as usual and from that moment the float acts as if it is fixed. You will need a float with a small bottom loop, or better still a special sliding float, which has a coil of wire for a loop fixed at right angles to the float. This ensures that the line slides through the float correctly every time.

The advantage of using a slider is that you do not have to worry about the distance between float and weight when you cast. In 15 ft of water the stop will be placed 15 ft or more above the weight. When you reel in, the stop slides through the rod rings, and flies out without catching when you cast. You can tie a short length of nylon on to the line to act as a stop, but a better bet is to use one of the tiny commercially produced line stops. You buy these ready threaded on to a loop of wire.

When you use a ready-threaded stop, don't slide the stop off the wire because you'll never be able to thread the line through it. Put the end of your reel line through the wire loop provided, double back the end of the reel line and hold it, and slide the stop down the wire and on to the line. And there it stays. If you take it off, you'll have to use another of the ready-threaded stops. These line stops are nicely shaped to slide easily through the rings when you cast, and are quite unbeatable. As with the fixed-float system you adjust the height of the float by altering the tension of the line.

A variation on the sliding-float system is to fish it with no stop on the line. This is not as awkward as it sounds, and has the advantage of your being able to position the float at any

59

point between you and the bait. You must ensure that the rod tip is below the surface when you tighten up, so the float ends up at the highest point in the line, and it will stop there, showing a perfectly good bite when you get one. You can even allow the float to slide right along the line so it is just beyond your rod tip, where you can see it easily. A very buoyant float should be used, and it should have the proper, long sliding ring at its base so that it slides easily.

With both sliding-float systems you must have a stop or a shot on the line 1 to 2 ft above the hook length to prevent the float sliding right down to the leger weight when you cast. A small leger stop, whose position can be easily adjusted, is a better bet than a shot, the weight of which will inevitably put a small dip in the line when you're fishing.

Tangles are much rarer than you may think, but if they happen continually it is probably due either to the float not being buoyant enough or to the bottom ring being either too small or too large – probably the latter. The only solution is to try with another float, preferably one with the special, long sliding ring. The best ones are commercially produced models, but few firms make them now. The first ones I used were by the late Billy Lane Jnr, who introduced the system to UK anglers, and then I had some excellent ones from Ultra Floats.

CHAPTER SIX

END RIGS AND KNOTS

The simplest leger rig consists of a drilled bullet running on the line, stopped by a split shot or a leger stop at a point above the bait. The distance between bait and bullet depends on whether you particularly want the bait to sink slowly during the latter part of its descent, and would normally be between 1–3 ft. This rig is not, in fact, particularly suited to presenting a slowly falling bait, and would normally be used on moving water, when the bullet's round shape rolls nicely along the bottom, allowing the angler to present a moving bait. However, it can be used on stillwaters, and has the advantage of allowing a 'straight through' rig to be used; that is, with the hook died direct to the reel line. This does away

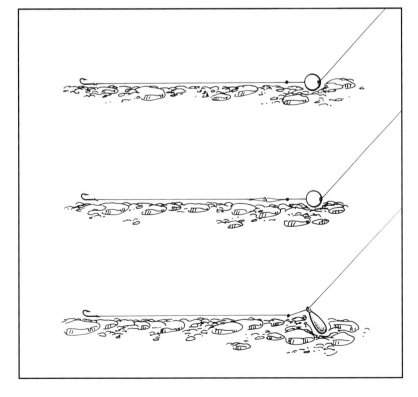

Three very basic rigs: top, the simplest drilled bullet rig with the hook whipped direct to the reel line, and a shot on the line; middle, a similar rig, but with a hook length looped to the end of the reel line; bottom, an Arlesey bomb is favoured on stillwaters as it is more streamlined for casting.

with all knots, except the one joining line to hook, and gives the strongest possible rig.

A variation is to put an Arlesey bomb on the line, also stopped above the bait with a shot. This is popular with carp anglers, and when the bomb is a big one it forms the basis of the 'bolt' rig – the fish runs for a few inches and then another shot, positioned above the weight, comes up against the weight and the fish hooks itself. This particular rig is used almost exclusively by carp anglers, and is not suitable for other species, which tend to feed much more timidly. The weight in this case needs to be quite heavy, to ensure that the fish hooks itself.

The basic rig, with just the lower shot or stop, is a perfectly workable rig on stillwaters. For the average angler, though, it is unsophisticated as the line can become twisted above the eye of the weight, in which case it would be acting as a dead weight and the fish would feel it as soon as it tried to swim off with the bait. On fast-running water it is a rig worth considering, however, as the shape of the Arlesey bomb gives it a tendency to lie still. Yet when the line is tightened, provided the bomb is the correct weight, it will roll round a little. This allows you to search the swim. The rig's simplicity and the fact that you can fish it 'straight through', as with the drilled bullet, makes it popular with specimen hunters. The biggest problem with a 'straight-through' rig is always the tendency of the heavy weight to knock a split shot down the line to the hook, so a leger stop is the usual, preferred method, as this holds the line quite tightly.

Paternosters

By far the most-used rigs are those based on the paternoster principle, in which the weight is tied to the end of the line and the hook is on a length of nylon attached somewhere above the weight. The hook length can be short, leaving the hook above the weight or, more usually, longer, putting the bait beyond the weight. The point at which they join can be

A sliding rig like this has the advantage that by moving the leger stop below the swivel the effective length of the hook snood can be altered in seconds. Inset, close-up of the set-up.

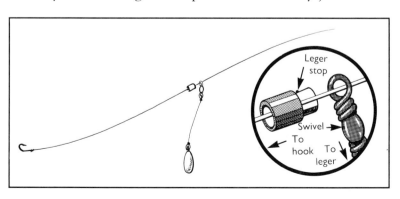

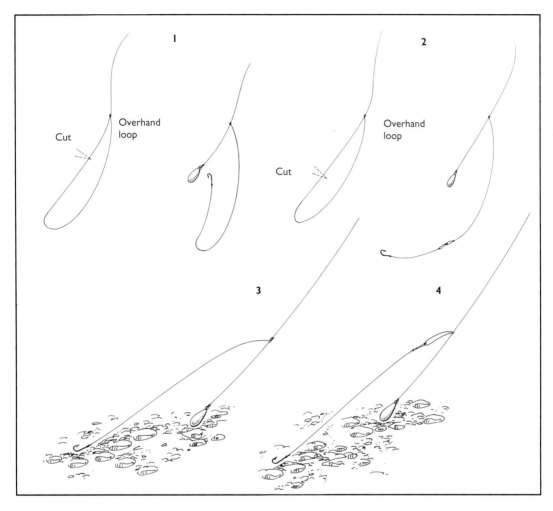

tied, or the weight can be on a short piece of nylon tied to a swivel running along the main line and stopped, as with the drilled bullet or Arlesey bomb, above the bait. To make this rig, the main line is threaded through a swivel, and then through the collar of a leger stop, and the hook whipped to the end of the line. Three feet above the hook the wedge of the leger stop is inserted into the collar, and this holds tight on the line; then 9 in of nylon are tied to the swivel, and the leger weight is tied to the other end of the nylon. As with the drilled-bullet rig a split shot can be used instead of the leger stop, but it can be difficult to get this to hold really tight on the line, although the new non-toxic shot are harder than the old-style lead shot and do, in fact, hold quite well.

Whether the join is tied or sliding is largely a question of personal preference. However, on stillwaters there seems no point in adding a swivel and perhaps a split shot if you are trying to get the bait to sink as slowly as possible – all that extra ironwork simply takes the rig down more quickly. And

Four simple leger paternoster rigs:
1: A loop is tied in the end of the reel line, cut, and the hook tied to one end and the leger weight to the other.
2: The same procedure is followed but a lighter hook length can be looped on.
3: A hook length is tied to the reel line with a water knot.
4: A loop is tied in the reel line above the weight and a hook length looped to this.

63

Above: Power Gum links have a snap swivel on the bottom, allowing you to change your leger weight or swimfeeder in seconds.

Above right: There are several types of leger weights. This one is flattened to hold bottom better in a flow.

there is also the possibility, particularly on stillwaters, that the line will snag the swivel as it sinks, so it will not run smoothly. However, if you especially want to fish a paternoster rig with the hook tied direct, with no knots in the line, then the sliding paternoster is your best option.

The weight can also be attached to a piece of Power Gum, which stretches when put under pressure and is popular with river anglers using a big weight to hold bottom. It absorbs some of the pressure of the strike, so the angler does not have to move the weight before he hits the fish. Power Gum has the advantage over elastic that it will stretch only a short way and that once stretched it retracts only slowly, without the typical springing-back you would get with elastic. For this reason it is also popular with fly anglers, who use it between fly line and leader to absorb the sudden smash strikes from big trout.

Instead of the swivel you can use one of the many little adaptor beads now on sale in tackle shops. A ready-made Power Gum link, complete with swivel on one end and a clip on the other to which the weight is attached, is also available. It was designed for use with swimfeeders, but can be used just as effectively with a leger weight.

There are several ways in which a fixed paternoster can be tied:

• By tying a large loop in the end of the reel line, using a simple double overhand knot, cutting this loop 9 in from the knot, and using the shorter end for the weight and the longer end for the hook (in this case, both hook length and reel line are the same strength).

• By using the above system but tying a small loop in the

64

end of the longer hook length to which a ready-tied hook, on thinner nylon, can be attached.

• By using a water knot, leaving 9 in of reel line and 3 ft or more of the thinner hook length.

• By tying the bomb to the end of the reel line and then tying a small loop 9 in above the bomb, to which a hook-to-nylon is attached.

There are other methods published from time to time in the angling press, but most are based on the above. It is worth experimenting until you find one you are happy with, though. Of the four, the last method is probably the easiest to tie, but slightly less neat. The third is the least easy to tie, since it involves learning the water knot. However, it is the neatest, and favoured by experienced leger anglers.

Tying the line instead of using a sliding system has advantages in moving water when there is weed or rubbish floating along, as it presents a much smaller spot where the weed can lodge when compared with a swivel and split shot, which picks up a lot of weed on occasions. This can not only cause the rig to stop sliding, but reduces its sensitivity and gives false bites in a current. For weedy swims on both still and running water there is no doubt that the tied paternoster rigs are to be preferred to the ones containing a swivel and stop.

There is one big advantage in using a sliding paternoster rig. By moving the position of the shot you can increase or decrease the hook length at will. And on occasions, when you are having trouble finding the best length it can be a real boon. At all times you should keep the swivel or sliding bead, and the leger stop, as small as possible.

With both fixed and running paternosters, the weight is normally on a piece of nylon around 4–6 in long. There is no real advantage to be gained in lengthening this as it only increases your chance of the hook length tangling in it.

Hook lengths

The length of the piece of nylon you use for the hook length is very important on the day, and probably the biggest single consideration once you have cast. Overall it's probably even more important than the bait you use, for it determines how the bait behaves, and how (and sometimes even whether) you will see your bites.

On running water in particular, and especially when using a swimfeeder, it can pay to go down to just a few inches, while on stillwaters a hook length of up to 6 ft might not be too much if you're aiming to present a slowly falling bait. If you can whip a spade-end hook direct to the end of a piece

65

of nylon you can start with a 6-ft hook length and gradually shorten it by cutting a foot or so off the end and re-whipping the hook to this, and repeating it until you find the optimum distance. Most stillwater anglers would aim to start with a 'drop' of about 3 ft. However, far too many anglers stick with their original choice all day instead of shortening it, or lengthening it, to experiment. Sometimes, even on stillwaters, a 12-in drop will take fish when a longer one won't.

If your hook length is of light nylon of 1½ lb or 1 lb breaking strain, and fished at a distance – say over 20 yd – it is as well to keep it at least 3 ft long if you can so that it stretches when you hit a fish. A 12-in piece of 1 lb line tied to a stronger reel line is liable to snap at the knot if you hit a big fish because it is not long enough to stretch much under pressure.

Carp anglers sometimes tie a short hook length a long way above the leger weight, so when the rig is tightened and the rod held in the air the bait is off the bottom. On shallow waters they tie the hook so far up the line that the bait can be held out of the water, then lowered so that it just touches the surface. The great advantage of this is that the fish can see no line going to the bait. At the moment it is a specialist rig, but it will, of course, take any surface-feeding species. It is easier to make this work in shallow waters, which is the carp's natural habitat in this country anyway.

One rig already mentioned briefly is the extra-long hook length used by carp anglers for fishing floating baits. There are several specialist match waters in this country that respond well to the tactic of catapulting out casters or floating maggots (maggots are made to float by keeping them in a tin in water for an hour or two), and fishing with a floating bait. In a 5-ft deep swim a leger rig containing a 6-ft hook length baited with a floating bait will allow you to fish your bait right on the surface, where carp will readily take it. This is a very effective method, for it allows you to get a floating bait out 50 yd or more and to ensure it stays there – freelined baits are inevitably blown out of the swim. Carp take these baits with such ferocity that there's hardly any need to watch the bait, as the rod is likely to be pulled off the rest.

On some waters – usually those holding ducks or wildfowl – floating baits are banned, and you should double-check whether the method is allowed before you employ it.

Knots

You have to tie knots, and here is a selection that should see you through. These are relatively easy to learn, but are not the definitive leger knots. By all means use others if you have confidence in them.

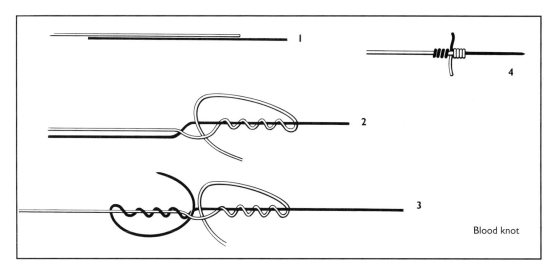

Blood knot

Blood knot

The usual knot to join two lengths of nylon is the blood knot. It is most likely to be used when you want to join a light hook length to the reel line without loops. You should always moisten line before drawing a knot tight as the heat generated when you pull a dry knot together can easily damage fine nylon.

Fisherman's knot

This is technically not as good as the blood knot, but it's never let me down, and I find it easier to tie. I use it to tie a

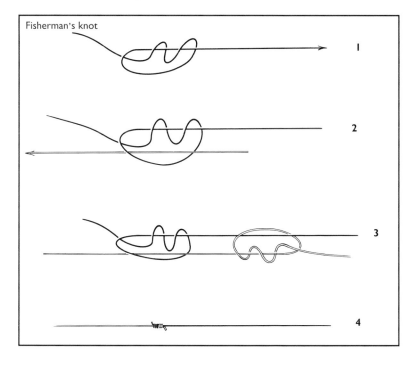

Fisherman's knot

Above:
Step 1: Lay both ends of line to be joined beside each other
Step 2: Twist one end four times round the other and tuck it between the two lines.
Step 3: Repeat with the other line, putting this end through the join from the opposite way to the first, but laying beside it.
Step 4: Moisten and draw tight by pulling the two main lines, not the ends. Trim.

Left:
Step 1: Tie a double hitch in one line.
Step 2: Push the other line through the loop formed.
Step 3: Tie a double hitch in this line round itself.
Step 4: Gently pull each loop tight, moisten, pull together and trim.

67

Step 1: Pass the end of the line through the swivel or eye of the hook.

Step 2: Make a large loop and lay it alongside the main line.

Step 3: Pass the end of the line round the loop and the main line four times

Step 4: Moisten and pull together.

Step 5: You can now trim the knot before pulling it tight to the swivel.

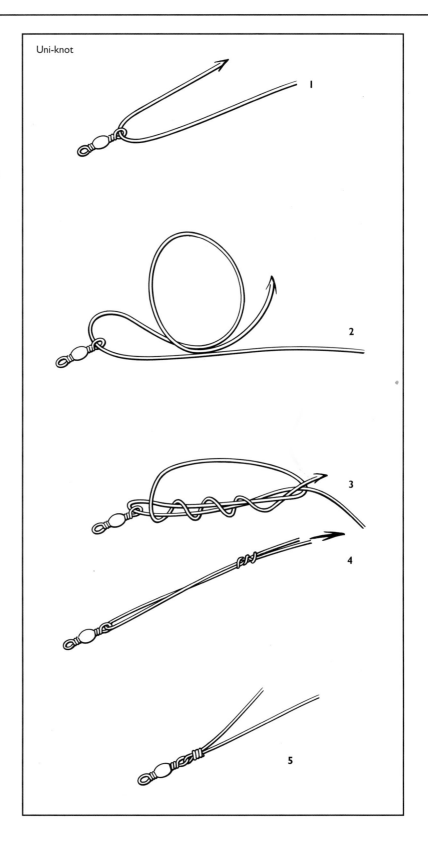

Uni-knot

68

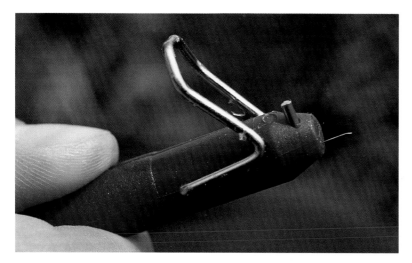

Hook-tying machines are very popular with anglers who find it difficult to whip on a small hook.

light hook length to a heavier reel line when I don't want any loops. I find it easiest to tie a double knot in the light line first, put the reel line through this, and pull the light line fairly tight. Then I complete the second part, moistening the two halves before pulling them together.

Uni-knot

This is the same basic knot as the grinner, and you may see it described as such. This is my knot for tying swivels to nylon for swimfeedering with a sliding paternoster. It can also be used for tying eyed hooks. The knot can be tightened to itself, the end trimmed, and then tightened down to the swivel. An extremely easy knot to tie.

Four-turn water knot

This is used to tie a hook length to the main line when fishing a fixed paternoster. It can also be used to join two lengths of

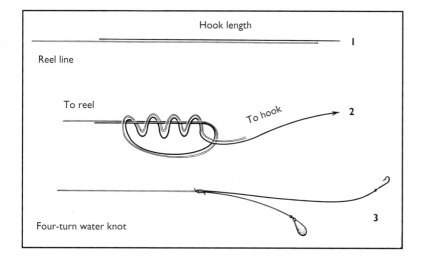

Four-turn water knot

Step 1: Lay your hook length so it overlaps the reel line by about 9 in.
Step 2: Hold the hook length against the main line at its top end and take both lines round itself four times, forming a loop as shown.
Step 3: Moisten and slowly pull the free ends together, while holding the top ends together. Your hook will normally be whipped to the longer end and your leger tied to the shorter end of reel line.

69

nylon. If you have trouble putting the longer end through the loop when it's windy, double it in half first.

Spade end knot

This is a very useful knot, enabling you to change a hook in seconds just by snipping it off and whipping another straight to the end of the hook length without breaking down the tackle. This is the knot I use for all my spade end hooks, holding the bend between the fingers of my left hand to tie it.

Step 1: Lay the line alongside the spade end and fold it back over itself, leaving a good loop at the end.
Step 2: Wind it back over the line and hook shank a minimum of four times and preferably seven or eight.
Step 3: Push the end back through the loop, ensuring it does not spring out.
Step 4: Start to tighten by pulling the main line, moisten, and finish tightening. Trim close.

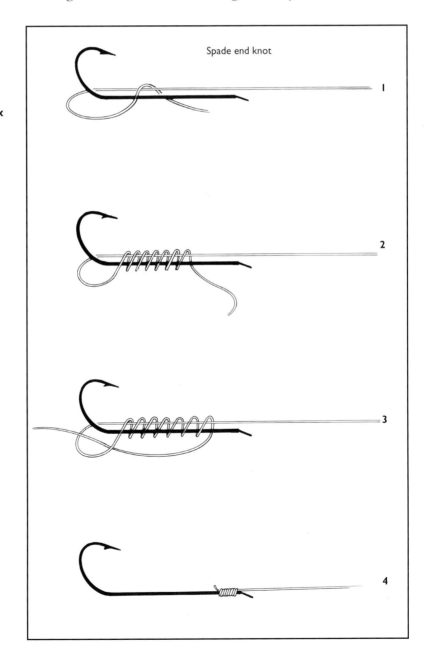

Spade end knot

70

Double overhand

The universal knot for tying a loop in the end of reel line or a hook length.

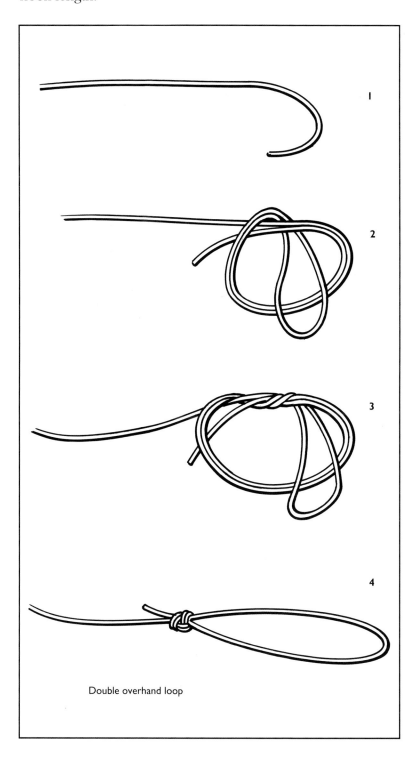

Double overhand loop

Step 1: Form a loop in the end of the line.
Step 2: Make a simple overhand loop by pushing the doubled end over itself.
Step 3: Repeat this so the end goes through the loop twice.
Step 4: You can manipulate the knot to alter the size of the loop slightly. Then moisten, pull tight and trim.

71

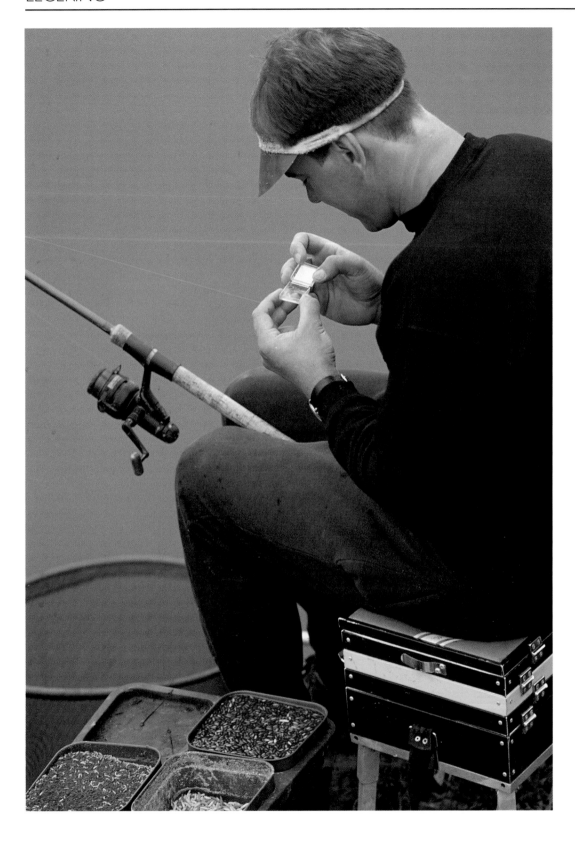

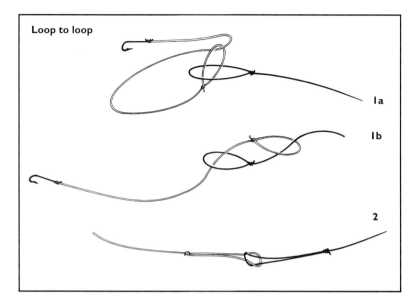

Loop to loop

1a

1b

2

Step 1a: Push the hook-length loop through the reel-line loop and push the hook through its own loop.

Step 1b: Alternatively, you can push the reel-line loop through the hook-length loop and push the hook through the reel line loop.

Step 2: Both methods will end up looking like the typical reef knot – though you may have to coax the knots through the loops as you pull tight. There is no need to moisten.

Far left: A good angler may change his hook several times during a day's fishing.

Loop to loop

The standard system for joining a ready-tied hook to the reel line. It can be taken apart and the hook used again if necessary. Although some books insist that there is a right and a wrong way of joining the loops, this is not so! The end result is the same whether you put the hook-length through the reel-line loop and the hook back through the hook-length loop (top); or whether you put the reel-line loop through the hook-length loop and the hook through the reel-line loop (centre). Just ensure the loops lie snugly, like a reef knot (bottom).

CHAPTER SEVEN

TIGHTENING AND TWITCHING

Moving the leger weight will cause the bait to move, which may prove attractive to fish. This is known as twitching the bait.

These are the two most important and perhaps most misunderstood and neglected aspects of legering. The way you tighten the line and move the bait is just as important to the leger angler as control of the tackle is to an angler using a stick float, and especially so if you're fishing a slowly-sinking bait. The line doesn't have to be tight to the weight for you to see a bite, but most anglers prefer it this way; while twitching the bait can have the same effect on a fish as a cornered mouse has on a cat – one movement and the cat pounces. It really can bring a lot more bites on occasions than leaving the bait static.

Sinking the line

The first thing to look at is the process of sinking the line after casting. And this is made much easier if it does not float. It helps to treat the line with washing-up liquid – this process is described in Chapter 1. A line that does not readily sink below the surface causes enormous problems, especially in windy weather, when a bow is inevitably formed when you cast. If the line sinks it can be tightened slowly without the leger weight being moved; but if it floats, you will not only take a lot of time tightening it, but will also be likely to move the leger weight while doing so. That in itself may not matter, but you may not be fishing in the place you think you are. The line is sunk either by twitching it by pulling and flicking the rod tip, or by plunging the rod tip well below the surface and reeling in with a series of short, sharp turns of the reel handle. Often you can see the line being pulled beneath the surface. You must be sure to get it properly sunk, otherwise the action of the waves will start giving you false bites.

In strong side winds you should always 'feather' the line (use your finger to control the speed with which it leaves the spool) while you cast, and stop the line coming off the spool as soon as the weight has hit the surface. This reduces the size of the bow that forms. If you can then push the rod under the surface as soon as you have cast, and before the weight hits the bottom, the line will sink much more quickly. You can keep a tight line as the weight sinks, which will ensure that the line, or at least most of it, will be below the surface by the time it has hit bottom, though the rig will inevitably kite towards you as it sinks. Then sink any remaining line by twitching or reeling in. So if you use this method overcast. The deeper the water, the more the rig will move forwards as it sinks.

Alternatively you can keep the rod tip below the surface but keep the bale arm open so the weight sinks vertically. Then you will have more line to sink by twitching and reeling in. Experienced anglers tend to prefer this latter method, but for the novice the first method is probably easier.

Tightening with a quivertip

The process of tightening should normally be done slowly. The reasons for this can be most easily explained by an imaginary situation on a lake. Let us assume you have a piece of bread flake on the hook and are after bream, using a quivertip rod, on a reasonably windy day. You've cast out using a 4-ft tail to give a slow sink. Immediately the bait has hit the water, push the rod tip under the surface to sink the

75

Bait pulled
down quickly

Line tightened
quickly

Most baits have a slow natural rate of fall which you should try to imitate. Bread flake is particularly buoyant, and a fish may watch it sink for some time (left). If you tighten the line (right) it will pull the bread quickly downwards and this may make fish, particularly bream, suspicious.

line between the rod and the point of entry. Watch the quivertip bend round as the weight sinks then flick back when the weight has hit the bottom. Now put the rod on the rest so that it's parallel to the water, but don't reel in yet! Let the line lie slack – it's against what most books will tell you, but the following is what happens.

As soon as you reel in, even a few inches, you will be pulling the line towards you, and on the end of that line is the bait. It will be falling reasonably naturally through the last 4 ft of water, and suddenly it will twitch and move quite unnaturally because it is being pulled towards you and down. Not only is this making the bait behave oddly, but it's reducing the amount of sinking time, which is short enough anyway.

There's another reason for tightening slowly that applies if there are bream in the swim. I have caught enough bream, and seen enough caught, to agree with some of the country's top bream anglers, who are sure a bream will watch a bait sink and then eye it on the bottom before making up its mind to eat it. An unnatural movement at that stage might put the fish off. Of course every bream angler knows that twitching a bait along the bottom can bring a response, but there will be plenty of time for that when the bait has been in the water a couple of minutes. You'll never go far wrong if you try to get the bait to sink as slowly as possible.

Once the bait has been out for a minute or two, it is time to start tightening the line. If you get a bite in the meantime – as the bait is sinking – you'll still see it as the line doesn't have to be tight to the quivertip. Even with a bow, it will bend round when a fish takes the bait.

Now tighten quite slowly, and each time you turn the reel the bait will twitch, even though the weight is not being moved, so you should be prepared for a bite even at this stage. Wind in until the quivertip is well bent, then stop, and watch the quivertip slowly straighten as it takes up the slack

76

Line remains
slack

Bait sinks naturally

line. Wait 15 seconds and repeat this. Keep repeating this operation until the quivertip won't straighten any more, and then wind backwards to give a little slack line until it straightens. A bite can come at any time, and is liable to be good, and unmissable – probably either a very slow bending of the quivertip after it has straightened, or a quick jerk or two as you reel in. You will probably strike instinctively at this latter bite, almost without realising you have done it.

Now – with the bait on the bottom and the line tight to the

Leaving the line slack after you have cast (left) will allow the bait to sink naturally. It may take 30–40 seconds, but still allow the line to lie slack (centre). Any fish which has watched it fall should now not be wary, and may take the bait. Be aware that tightening the line will cause the bait to move, even if you do not move the weight!

Left: When you pull the line, it's easiest to grip it between the reel and the first ring.

leger weight – the time to start pulling the bait towards you. This is not only creates the right movement, but also makes little puffs of mud spurt up from the weight as it is moved. However, a piece of bread flake can easily be pulled off, so the twitching trick should be kept until you've a worm or a maggot on. If you have a heavy bait on the hook, like a worm, you can begin to tighten after, perhaps, 30 seconds. Even then, however, it's often a good idea to leave it as long as you dare.

With a really big bow in the line after casting you will have to tighten more quickly – not because you won't see the bites, but because you won't be able to hit the fish on the strike. On water which is moving, the line will tighten itself, of course, and the faster the current, the more quickly you will see the quivertip bend. Then you tighten the line by winding in and waiting until the quivertip has resumed its normal bend before repeating the excercise. Inevitably on moving water there will be a bow, and provided it's not a huge one it should make little difference to your ability both to see bites and hook the fish. In fact, leaving a big bow will help a light weight hold bottom more easily.

The twitch – quivertip

Let's assume you have a single maggot on, in the lake swim, and have tightened as described – nice and slowly over a period of a couple of minutes. The length of time you wait before starting to move the bait is optional, and some bream anglers will leave it 10 or 15 minutes. I've never been that patient!

There are several ways of twitching. The one I favour is to reel in about a turn, until the quivertip is bent right round. Then take the line between reel' and butt ring and pull it towards you until the tip springs back straight. Let go of the line in your hand, and reel in until just a small amount of slack is left. Usually the drift on the water will inch this line through the rod rings and put just a slight bend in the quivertip. An alternative method is to reel in and watch the quivertip bend right round and then spring back. Then reel in until the tip is almost straight. A third option is to lift the rod and pull the weight along the bottom, and then replace the rod on the rest and tighten.

Bites will frequently come as you tighten, and you will suddenly realise that there is resistance. This makes it difficult to know exactly when to strike, of course. The best bites are those which occur just after the tip has been allowed to straighten, and drift is tightening the line. Then the line will suddenly be seen to tighten more quickly, and the tip will just bend round in an almost-unmissable bite.

78

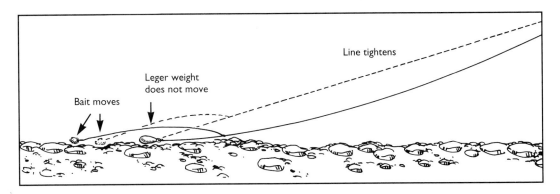

The violin pluck

This was a term coined by Cambridge matchman, Percy Anderson, and is a surprisingly effective little dodge. It involves no more than pulling the line tight, so the quivertip pulls round, and then letting it go, without the leger weight actually moving. The drift will take up the slack line and tension the tip again. The tiny movement of the line seems to impart a tremble to the bait, and will frequently bring a bite. On narrow waterways, or where the fish seem to be concentrated in a small area, this is a useful trick, as it doesn't pull the bait out of the swim. Experienced anglers will allow a little more slack line out each time they pull, which gradually takes longer to tighten. Then they will reel in so the excess slack line is taken up (you get a lot of bites at this point), and start the sequence again.

The violin pluck – just tightening the line upwards in slack water can cause the bait to move.

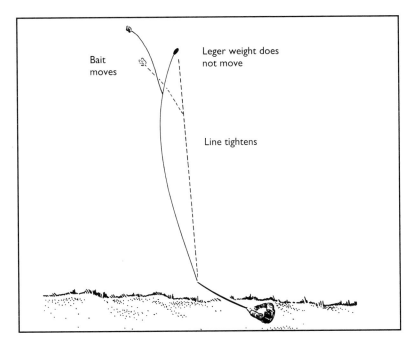

The violin pluck in moving water – tightening the line against the current will also cause the bait to move.

79

Above: A beautiful summer's day, when fish are likely to come up in the water and take baits as they fall.

Right: Don't be in too much of a hurry to tighten your line if you want to catch bream like this.

80

You need to set the clutch exactly right when you strike into a good fish, and to make sure the anti-reverse is off when you are about to net it.

Tightening with a swingtip

Sinking the line when using a swingtip is done in the same way as with every other method – by plunging the rod tip beneath the waves and reeling in. The swingtip then gives the advantage of allowing better bite indication as the bait is sinking than the quivertip does. You'll see bites on both, but the swingtip has a potentially greater distance to move, so it's easier to see the bite develop.

After the line has been sunk, the rod is placed on the rest and the reel turned until the swingtip is out straight (or at least as straight as it will go). Then it is allowed to fall back until it's vertical to the water; and this process is repeated until the tip stays at an angle to the surface, when some slack line is let out until it's vertical or almost so. Most swingtip anglers like it to rest at a slight angle from the vertical as this readily shows drop-back bites. The swingtip will tend to take up the slack line more slowly than a quivertip, and you will get many bites as it is sinking back. These range from a rocket-like lift to a little tremble. However, because the swingtip is larger than the quivertip most anglers find it easier to watch. The longer the swingtip, the more line it will take up on each drop, and the fewer number of times you will have to reel in. This decreases the chance of getting a bite as you are reeling in – the most difficult bites to spot and hit.

81

The twitch – swingtip

The options are the same as with the quivertip: reel in until the tip is straight, then pull the line above the reel until the tip drops down, finally reeling in to take up the slack. Or keep winding until the tip straightens and drops back. Or lift the rod and pull until you feel the leger weight move. In all cases, you judge the tension of the line by the angle the swingtip makes with the surface, always remembering that not all swingtips will naturally hang straight down, of course.

Other indicators

Whatever indicator you use the method of tightening the line will be the same, although the twitching may vary slightly. With a butt indicator you will find that slack line may not be so easily taken up by drift or flow because of the increased friction between line and rod rings. With slack lining the opposite happens, and you may find that the drift takes the line quite straight, and you can't see bites so well. In that case you will either have to change to a quivertip or a swingtip, or you can fix a butt indicator, weighted if necessary to take up the slack line.

Size of the leger weight

The lighter the weight, the easier you will find it to move. However, in a wind a lighter weight will be less accurate to cast, and will be moved more easily as you tighten if there is a bow. It won't take you long to work out whether you are moving the weight as you tighten up, so you should take a range of weights, say ⅛ oz, ¼ oz, ⅜ oz (a very useful size), ½ oz, and ¾ oz. Be prepared to change them if necessary so that you get the best compromise between accuracy of casting and ease of twitching. If you have a link into which you can clip the weight you will be more likely to change it if necessary. Aim to get the lightest weight that will hold still as you tighten up. The one exception to this is when you're fishing in a swim holding a lot of bottom weed. In that case, when you have found a clear patch and are sure you can cast right on to it, you may be advised to increase the weight of the leger to ensure you don't drag the bait out of position as you tighten. The same advice applies in running water.

Striking

A word of warning: bites resulting from twitching the bait are liable to be be fierce, and you should try to restrain yourself from reacting in the same way. Every season, anglers twitching a bait, with their hand already on the rod, see their quivertip hurtle round. They strike hard, either breaking their hook length, pricking the fish, or taking the bait out of its lips. Few fish are lost by the angler striking too softly – lots are lost by striking too fast or hard. So take your time.

The correct way to approach any strike, particularly when a big fish like a bream or a tench is the quarry, is to 'lean into the fish'. It can be misleading to watch a Fenland bream angler give a huge strike over his head, for he may simply be taking up slack line and then reducing the power when he feels the fish. At the same time, he will be trying to get the fish moving immediately to separate it from the shoal. It's a complicated combination of actions he is performing, all in what appears to be just one sweep.

For your first efforts, don't try to emulate the experienced bream angler. He may have 20 years of experience, doing it weekend after weekend. Just try to lean into the fish to begin with, no matter what its size, and then keep a tight line. The rest will come naturally.

It's essential to set the clutch of a fixed-spool reel so it gives line if you hit something big. Not only does this prevent the line from breaking on the strike, but it tells you immediately that there is extra pressure on the clutch. This is especially useful in windy weather, when it can sometimes be difficult to judge the size of a fish you are playing.

Playing a fish

Most fish caught in this country can be played without giving line from the reel. So the favourite method of striking is to click on the anti-reverse and rely on the clutch giving if you hook an extra-big fish. Then you simply click off the anti-reverse, and give line by back-winding if this proves necessary. However, if you are fishing for carp, big tench or barbel, you may find the first run of these immensely powerful fish is so fast that either you can't click the anti-reverse off in time, or if you do the reel spins backwards so fast that you can't control it. Either way, there is great danger of the line breaking. In these cases, it is essential to play the fish on the clutch, or with a combination of the clutch and some backwinding. You should set the clutch a little lighter than you would normally do, and hold the spool with you finger when you strike. Many anglers use reels with the drag adjuster on the back of the reel, as these can be altered in a split second while the fish is still running, just by turning the knob. Reels with the drag on the spool are much more difficult to adjust during a fight, although they are still popular with matchmen, as the spool can be tightened right down.

83

CHAPTER EIGHT

LEGERING FOR BREAM

Big and golden – fish like this are worth taking a bit of trouble over.

If you have never legered, or are not sure whether you have been doing it correctly, it will do no harm to take an imaginary fishing trip, so you get a feel for what legering is all about. The target will be bream on a Fen drain, since of all the species normally caught by legering, bream can be the most frustrating, and need the most care to be taken.

Venue – Fen drain
Width – 20 yd
Depth – 14 ft in middle
Conditions – strong wind from right
Time of year – summer

84

It's on a water like this that legering can give an advantage over any other method. No matter where the fish are, you can get the bait to them. Floatfishing will be difficult in this wind, and if the fish are under the far bank, as they most probably will be, they will be out of range of all but the longest poles, which will be impossible to handle in this wind anyway. So a leger it is.

If you're after big fish don't risk using fine-wire hooks - feeder hooks like this are a much better bet.

The first job is to find a spot for the tackle box, preferably somewhere that has some sort of cover like reeds on the far bank. Having done that, decide how to sit – back to the wind is most comfortable, especially if it rains! Many Fen drains have a road along one bank, with open farmland on the other side. And you can bet your boots that when it's dredged, as these drains are every few years, the dredger works on the far bank to avoid holding up traffic and so that it can dump the dredged muck from the drain behind it. So the deeper water is almost invariably towards the side opposite the road. That means fishing towards the far bank, as bream tend to make for the deepest water. And the wind is ideal – bream feed more confidently when there's a good disturbance on the surface.

One point to watch is that all Fen drains have a natural direction of flow, even though they are normally regarded as stillwaters. The natural direction is the way they move when water is let out into the sea. If the wind is blowing in this direction, as it is today, prospects are good; if the wind is opposite to the natural direction of flow the bream will probably not feed.

The first decision is whether to use a quivertip or a swingtip. I will choose a swingtip because it's a fair depth here, and there may be bites 'on the drop'. In any case, the quivertip can be used later when fishing with a swimfeeder. The rig could be a straight drilled bullet with the line running through the centre, but this isn't ideal for presenting a slowly dropping bait. So it's a paternoster rig. First, however, some rod rests have to be set up so that the swingtip, which is about 10 in long, will touch the water when it hangs vertically. One rest is positioned about 18 in from the tip, another one under the handle, near the box, and one in the middle to steady the rod against the wind.

Choose a 3-lb reel line, and tie a 4-ft length of 2-lb line 10 in from the end, using the water knot shown earlier. To this, whip a size 16 forged hook (those with a short shank are preferable if you can get them). On the end of the reel line tie a swivel link, and clip a ⅜ oz Arlesey bomb to it for weight. This is heavy enough to give accuracy in this wind, but small enough to twitch along the bottom if necessary. The best bait is a nice juicy redworm – roll it on your knee for a second or

85

two to make it easier to hook.

Cast the tackle just over half way across the drain and plunge the rod tip under the water, leaving the bale arm open, to sink some of the line. You'll know when the weight has hit bottom as the swingtip will stop jerking, Now check that the line has all sunk. If you look closely you can see a bit lying on the surface in the middle of the drain; reel in a couple of times very quickly. Now it should be beneath the waves. Put the rod in the rest and wind in until the swingtip is out straight. It immediately starts falling back; when it has dropped back to a vertical position wait a second or two and wind in until it's out straight again. It drops back again. Repeat this process until it doesn't drop back properly. You may get a bite during this time if a fish decides to take the sinking bait – if so, it will probably be a nice gentle lift. The tip will probably rest at an angle of about 45°, so back-wind until it's vertical, and switch on the anti-reverse.

The reason for casting only half-way is that it's advisable not to cast right into a shoal of bream if you can help it. They are likely to be within 6 ft of the far bank, so cast short to begin with, and increase the distance with each cast.

Groundbait

This could have been mixed first, but there's a great temptation to start throwing it in quickly if you do that. The 10 to 15 minutes spent mixing it now will allow you to check whether there are fish already in the swim by seeing whether you get any bites or line bites caused by fish accidently hitting the line. If there are signs of fish, or if you hook a bream, catapult casters out to keep the fish interested. If there are no bites at all use the groundbait.

Into the bowl go two or three cupfuls of proprietary groundbait designated as being for rivers or lakes, the same amount of white breadcrumbs, and a cupful of groundbait containing crushed hemp. Mix it together well by stirring, and add a little water – about an eggcupful. Mix this up for at least a minute – it's obviously too dry, but mix it well. Now add a little more water and re-mix thoroughly for another minute. It's still too dry, but you are ensuring that the water is mixed evenly through it, which is very important. Each mix should take at least a minute. After four or five eggcupfuls of water, the groundbait will hold together well with one squeeze, and can be left for five minutes.

There's been no indication on the swingtip, so re-cast a bit further out. The worm has not been touched, so keep it on. This time aim for three-quarters of the way across, sink the line and re-set the swingtip. The drift caused by the wind is lifting the swingtip a bit, but – any bite will still be visible.

Back to the groundbait, which is still absorbing the water and is drier than before. It needs a little more water. A garden spray can be used to add water in minute amounts, or the bowl can be dipped in the water. A good tip here, if you are in a precarious position that makes it dificult to get down to the water, is to dip your landing net in the water. When you lift it out it will still have water hanging in the folds, and you can shake this over the groundbait bowl. An even better idea is to carry a sponge, which allows you to squeeze as much, or as little, water into the groundbait as you wish. Mix the groundbait well, until it will hold together easily when squeezed, and add some squatts.

Checking for fish

Now comes one of the most important tasks of the day: getting groundbait out. There hasn't been a bite, so retrieve and check the bait, which appears not to have been touched. However, a new worm will not hurt, so put one on, and cast right across, to within 4 ft of the far bank. Set the swingtip, and turn your attention to the groundbait. Add just a few casters in one spot, and mix these in lightly, grabbing a couple of handfuls of groundbait and forming them into an orange-sized ball. Squeeze hard – you must be certain it won't break up when you throw it – and wet the throwing hand to make the release cleaner. Now throw it out to within 6 ft of the far bank. If you can throw it underarm so much the better, as this may make it more accurate.

When the groundbait hits the surface watch the swingtip. This is vitally important. If there are bream out there they will probably be upset by the sound of the splash and start moving around in a slight panic, and one may hit the line. Nothing has happened, so mix up another ball and put this in roughly the same place. You can follow a groundbaiting pattern, but this needs accurate throwing. The beginner is better off just getting it all into the same spot, although an easy pattern is described in Chapter 11.

Watch the swingtip as this second ball hits the surface. Suddenly it flicks up and drops straight back. That was certainly a line bite and warns us that there are fish – probably bream – out there. To put in more groundbait now will panic the shoal further, so be patient. Leave the tackle where it is and wait – a most difficult thing to do when we know there are fish there.

Five minutes have gone by and there's been no further indication. Either the fish have gone, or they have settled down again. Try a twitch, which will move the bait slightly and may cause a fish to attack it. Grasp the line between the reel and the first ring and pull it back towards you. The tip

87

Left: Always add water to groundbait – never the other way round
Below left: Mix for at least two or three minutes, preferable for five minutes.
Below right: The balls should hold together without too much squeezing.

rises; keep pulling, and the rod tip will bend round; keep pulling and suddenly the rod tip will straighten as the weight is moved. Now leave the slack line as it is, and it will slowly tighten in the drift.

The tip rises slightly as the drift picks up the line, but keeps on rising, quite quickly, until it is out straight. It's much higher than the drift has taken it before, so this must be a bite. Strike! Not ridiculously hard, but very firmly, over your left shoulder. The strike is across your body, because you are facing to the left, and it's not quite so easy to control as it would be if you were facing to the right.

The rod bends as if you have hit the bottom. Hold it tight and keep leaning back against the fish. The aim is to get it out of the shoal before it realises it's hooked. Now it's running away to the left, and threatening to take line from the reel. Knock off the anti-reverse and play the fish by back-winding when you have to, and retrieving line when you can. It's definitely a good bream – you can tell by the way it keeps nodding its head as it starts to swim away, hence the slang term 'nodder' used by many Fenland anglers.

You must be patient now! It will probably take about five minutes to beat this fish, and firm pressure is all you need

until it comes towards the side, as it is doing now. Its golden flanks flash and it looks a lot bigger than a dinner plate. Now it's making short rushes near the side, and this is the danger time. Don't put your landing net in yet, just ensure that it's handy by your left side. More than one bream has been lost when the fish has dived under the submerged net and tangled the line in the mesh.

Above left: A spray is useful for adding tiny amounts of water from time to time.

If the fish wants to run out towards the centre of the drain let it do so, it will be easier to bring in, in one long pull. Now it's gone again, and suddenly comes to the surface and lies on its side. Try to keep its head up, slightly out of the water, and it should be yours. Draw it in slowly, still keeping its head up, and when you have it on the correct length of line put the net in, and pull the fish over it in one smooth movement. Never scoop with the net. This fish, about 5 lb, is coming nicely; over the net; and lift.

Above right: Before throwing in a ball like this always wet your hands and pat down the surface so it holds together in flight.

Keeping the shoal

The problem now is how to keep the shoal in position without panicking the fish. The obvious choice is to catapult loose casters out. However, if the wind is just too strong to loose-feed, and you feel you have to use groundbait, don't do it yet. Wait until the fish have been in position for at least half an hour, and are feeding confidently, before you risk scaring them. While they grub around picking up your bait they are also disturbing the natural insect life in the bottom, and could stay here feeding all day.

Today you can just about get come casters out to the shoal, but if the wind increases you will be in trouble. However, don't panic – take your time re-tackling, slide all the slime off the hook length (bream are slimy fish) and re-cast. Only this time don't risk going right into the shoal. Cast just over half way across, and try to pick off the fish on the outskirts of the shoal as this causes less disturbance to the main shoal.

Send the bait out again, sink the line, and tighten the tip for

89

When bream fishing always try to avoid casting into, or beyond, the main shoal if possible.

Catch fish anywhere in the shaded area

ANGLER

the first time. This time, before the tip has dropped back to the vertical position, it flicks and rises again very slowly. Suddenly its speed picks up and it is pulled out absolutely straight. It's another bite, and you've already hooked it. The fish certainly took that as the bait dropped. These first few seconds are vital – if you lose a fish in the shoal there is a good chance the rest will scatter. So hold it tight and let it cruise away – in any direction – out of the shoal. Now the rod is really bent, and you're on your way to a good catch.

You'll find fish in your swim as quickly as this only infrequently in a match, because they tend to be disturbed by anglers tramping along the bank. However, when you're pleasure fishing it's not uncommon. And on this occasion you made your own luck by stopping the groundbait going in as soon as you saw an indication. It's useful to cast right across to the far bank before you put the first groundbait in, as this gives you a better chance of having a fish hit the line. If you had cast half way, the fish could have moved around without ever hitting the line.

When you have three or four fish in your net, you'll have to decide whether to add more groundbait or to carry on as you are, wait till the shoal moves off, and then put in a big load to start them feeding again if they come back. On the whole, I favour the latter, following the advice of one of the best bream anglers in the Fens, former National Champion Bryan Lakey, to: 'Never groundbait on top of a feeding shoal of bream'. If you do, then putting in golf-sized pieces makes a lot less disturbance than bigger ones.

Matchfishing

Many anglers make the mistake of treating bream differently in a match to the way they do when pleasure fishing. However, they are the same fish – the only difference is that they are likely to be finicky because of the disturbance, and may be moved around quite a lot by anglers hooking and losing them or disturbing the feeding shoals by groundbaiting on their heads. That means they may move through your swim two or three times during the day. The main difference is that if you think bream may feed at some time during the match, you should be sure to get enough feed in during your first bombardment to keep the shoal interested if they stop and – even more important – enough to give you confidence to carry on fishing without continually topping it up with more balls. If the fish happen to be in the swim, as they were in our imaginary session, stop groundbaiting immediately and concentrate on the fishing.

Your tactics may, in fact, be dictated by the anglers close to you, and if they put in a load of groundbait you will probably have to follow suit. For the one thing you don't want is to be sitting there with nothing in your swim when a shoal, perhaps disturbed by anglers groundbaiting further down the line, decides to stop in your area. If they start to feed nearby and you throw in a a lot groundbait, you will probably scare them away, and as well as ruining your own chances you will be decidedly unpopular with your neighbours. In 35 years of matchfishing I can't remember a single occasion when the fish have moved to the swim of an angler doing this. If you are caught out your best bet is to try to loosefeed, or to use a groundbait feeder, or don't feed at all. I have known several occasions when anglers not putting in any groundbait have caught bream. After all, frequently the bream stop in an

91

Above: If you're getting line bites sit with your arms folded so you are not tempted to strike.

Right: Watch your tip when you play a fish – and concentrate.

unoccupied peg just because there's no disturbance there!

Also remember that weights in a match are rarely massive, and you will probably be looking at only six fish to win, and a couple to get you in the money. If it's one of those days when the fish just will not stop feeding, you will be better off concentrating on catching as many as you can, not continually mixing up groundbait. Then, if the fish move away, get in plenty more feed in one big operation, and hope they return.

The five pointers to successful matchfishing for bream are (in order of importance):

- Fish for bream and stick to it.
- Don't groundbait on top of a feeding shoal.
- Don't aim too high.
- Don't rush your striking.
- Take your time and get them in the net.

92

CHAPTER NINE

THE OPEN-ENDED SWIMFEEDER

The swimfeeder has made an enormous impact on angling in Britain in the past 30 years, and deservedly so, as it helps the angler get his bait out to the spot where he is fishing without fail. It was introduced to a sceptical angling fraternity by Londoners, who had been using it for many years, and has been refined to such a degree that there is now not only a whole range of swimfeeders, but also a range of groundbaits for them. The two main types available are block-end, which has plastic caps on both ends, and the open-end, also known as a groundbait feeder, on which the ends are open. There is also the very versatile frame feeder and variations on this.

All types of swimfeeder can be used with all the indicators already mentioned, though in medium-to-fast running water a purpose-built feeder rod will usually have to be used. With this you will see the bites on the rod tip, which acts in the same way as a quivertip.

As for choosing which feeder to use, an open-ended feeder must have its ends plugged with groundbait, which slowly disintegrates and allows the contents to form a little heap on the bottom, so this is the usual choice for stillwater; and a block-end is usually filled just with maggots which crawl through the holes in the side and in the ends, and is the usual choice for running water. Block-ends are, however, frequently used for stillwater fishing and are marginally the more versatile of the two types, especially ones that have two easily removeable end caps, allowing them to be converted to open-end feeders in seconds.

Frame feeders are a new introduction. Groundbait is squeezed around the cage-like feeder and disintegrates quickly once it hits the water. These are used almost exclusively by stillwater anglers. There is also the cage feeder – a type of open-ended feeder made of wire instead of plastic.

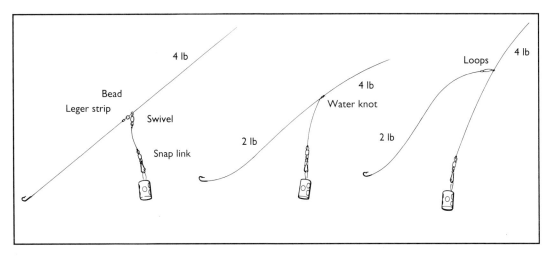

Rigs

Rigs for swimfeeders are basically the same as for the straight leger, with the option of using fixed or sliding paternosters, and with the block-end feeder the option of running the line straight through the middle – the equivalent of the simple drilled bullet rig. As with the straight leger, anglers use a paternoster nine times out of ten. On stillwaters or slow rivers the fixed paternoster is most popular, while on fast waters the sliding rig has some advantages. At all times, the advice to keep it simple is of paramount importance, always remembering that a swimfeeder exerts more pressure on rod and line, and a hooked fish, than a straight leger rig, so tackle tends to be slightly stronger than that which would be used by an angler legering in the same conditions.

Probably of more importance for the inexperienced leger angler than the exact rig used is when, and how, to use a swimfeeder, and which sort to choose.

Open-end feeders

Shop-sold models are usually made from clear plastic, and have no ends. The various makes have all sorts of different fittings to attach them to the line. For the beginner it makes little difference which fitting you choose, so long as you are confident you are seeing bites. However, once you are familiar with using feeders of any kind you should pay some attention to this point, particularly if you have experienced any tangling of the hook length round the link connecting the feeder to the line. They all have holes along the side, though these are not, in fact, strictly necessary, and some top anglers use home-made feeders without holes because they plane towards the surface when you retrieve them, bringing them

Typical swimfeeder paternoster rigs:
Left: the very strong 'straight-through' rig, which has no knots in it. The bead is optional.
Centre: the neat water knot rig.
Right: the easily-tied double-loop set-up. The snap link allows quick changes of swimfeeder to be made.

95

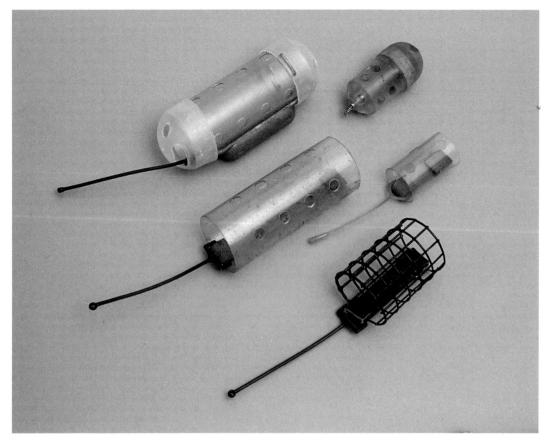

Swimfeeders, from the top: large and small block-ends; large and small open-ended feeders; a new-style cage feeder.

over any snags and also over the heads of any feeding fish.

Any feeder can be tied to the line paternoster-style or allowed to run on the main line. For the beginner, a running swivel will allow you to experiment with the length of the hook drop, which is important on both still and moving waters. To alter the effective hook length you just push the swivel stop (the purpose-made leger stop is probably best) up the line.

For a fixed paternoster you would use a water knot, using a lighter line for the hook length than the reel line. Most authorities say you should use a four-turn water knot, but I usually manage only two turns and it's never let me down yet! As with a straight leger, it is as well to begin with a good hook length – 3–4 ft – as it is easy to shorten it if necessary, but not so easy to lengthen it.

The open-end feeder tends to be reserved for stillwaters or slowly moving rivers. In fast water the groundbait is quickly dispersed, and here a block-end would be the usual choice. The best use for an open-ended feeder in fast water is probably to get sweetcorn or cubes of luncheon meat out to the swim, using a very big feeder plugged at each end with stiff groundbait. On one fast Trent backwater I always set up a big feeder rod with a big open-ended feeder just for this purpose, and don't always even put a hook on it. Four or five quick casts is all I need to get a fair load of luncheon meat out into the swim.

However, it's on stillwaters, where there are roach and bream, where the groundbait feeder comes into its own. You can either fill it with a mix of cereal groundbait and maggots or casters, or you can plug it firmly with groundbait at one end, pour your bait into the middle, and plug the other end. This latter takes longer, but is particularly good for getting worms into the swim. Most anglers mix squats or casters with the cereal and fill the feeder with the mixture, pinching the groundbait firmly between finger and thumb when it's in the feeder so it doesn't fall out during the cast.

LAKE FISHING

To illustrate the way you use a groundbait feeder, let us look at an imaginary situation on a lake:

Depth – 15 ft at 30 yd out
Wind – strong from the side, but warm
Season – late summer

Bream are big fish, and there's a greater chance of a big swimfeeder hitting one on its side, and scaring it, than a leger weight, which is much smaller.

97

Locals have told you that the bream will probably be 30 yd out. And since you can't loose-feed you must get your casters and squatts out some other way – either in balls of groundbait put out with a catapult, or thrown out, or in a feeder. The wind makes throwing out of the question, so you have a choice between catapult or feeder. On any big water when a strong wind is blowing, accuracy with a catapult may be affected, and in 15 ft of water the groundbait must be pretty hard to get to the bottom without starting to disperse, because there will also be quite a strong drift, which will take any loose groundbait and casters or squatts to one side, out of the swim. The drift will, in fact, probably be the opposite way to the wind because on big waters a strong undertow can develop. You can't be sure of this, however, so there will be a lot of guesswork involved. If you are confident that you can mix your groundbait so it won't break up until it nears the bottom, and think you can put it accurately into place with a catapult, then you can fish over it with a straight leger. But if you are not sure of your abilities, then a groundbait feeder is the perfect answer. It will always take your groundbait to the spot you are casting to.

First job, even before you put your tackle together, is to mix some groundbait. The proprietary brands produced especially for swimfeeders are excellent. However, the mixing is so important that it is worth a section on its own.

Mixing groundbait

The basic principle of mixing up cereal into a groundbait is covered in Chapter 8, and there's more advice in Chapter 11. However, each day requires a slightly different approach, and in these conditions you need a fairly dry mix that will hold together well when squeezed once, tightly, in your hand. It will be slightly wetter than that used by, say, pole anglers who are only throwing it out a few feet from the side and expect it to break up as soon as it hits the surface. The mix for the feeder must stay intact until the tackle gets to the bottom. Experience will tell you when you have the mixture right – better still, check with an experienced angler, who will know instinctively when the consistency is right. For this swim it is better to err on the side of getting it too hard, so it gets right down, rather than too soft so it comes out when the feeder hits the water. White breadcrumbs need to be added to the main ingredients, as these tend to stiffen the mix, (brown breadcrumbs make it softer).

Many books tell you to sieve the groundbait as well, but for bream this is rarely necessary, although it does help get all the lumps out. However, the extra-large crumbs give them something to eat, and won't fill them up, so don't worry about them. When you are more experienced you may be happier using a sieve, as this does make the groundbait more consistent in its texture.

As always, add water in tiny amounts and mix thoroughly each time. When you think you have the consistency right, try it in a feeder. Pinch the ends to see if the groundbait holds in well, even when you drop the feeder back into the bowl from a height. If it does, leave it and tackle up. You will be amazed at how much the groundbait is going to dry out in the next 15 minutes, so be prepared to add a little more water when you start fishing, especially as you are going to add squatts and casters, and the groundbait will need to bind together even better to hold these in. Don't add any maggots to the groundbait yet.

This may seem time-consuming, but it is probably the biggest single factor that separates the competent but unsuccessful angler from the successful ones, whether you're floatfishing, leger fishing or using a pole. It really is that important. Years ago I used to sling in the groundbait, add one lot of water, and fish with whatever resulted. There was more excuse then, since we had only breadcrumbs, maize and a few other items available. Now there is no excuse, because modern packeted groundbaits are superb. Several times in a season I will tip a bowl of accidently over-wetted groundbait into a polythene bag to take home, and mix up a fresh batch to fish with. Mixed groundbait will freeze down, so nothing is wasted. Mixing dry groundbait into a batch of over-wet groundbait will not solve the problem, as it takes so long for the two to absorb the same amount of moisture.

First you must decide on the mix of cereals you are going to use, and you can only arrive at that by experiment or by taking advice. If in doubt, get advice from the top matchmen because they really know their stuff. Go to one of the many roadshows or talks that take place all over the country. The Ian Heaps talk at the 1987 Chatsworth Angling Fair was nothing short of brilliant: two wineglasses of this (he was showing off – you can use a vacuum flask top), one wineglass of that, and one wineglass of another, mix for five or ten minutes telling jokes and adding water very slowly, and hey presto, you have a ball of groundbait you can throw from one spectator to another across the tent. And they did! Ian also had a glass tank there so you could see how that particular combination of ingredients behaved underwater, and how long it took to break up. You don't have to suffer Ian's jokes, as this sort of advice is given regularly in *Improve Your Coarse Fishing*. Make a note of the various mixes and find one – just one – you are happy with for legering. Don't confuse yourself. And forget about taste and smell to begin

99

Right: Sieve the groundbait, or rub it between your hands, to get rid of the lumps.

Below: Squatts are the best all-round maggot for putting in your groundbait.

with, although you can add small amounts of powder or liquid additive if you feel confident about them. Concentrate on texture. You will be amazed at how your catches improve when you get it just right.

Use fingers and thumb to fill an open-ended feeder.

Tackle

As the wind is so strong, in the sample situation, we will choose a medium-sized feeder with ¼–½ oz of lead in a strip down the side. When groundbait is added it will weigh more, of course, and should carry the 30 yd to the swim fairly easily. And because bream are finicky feeders, tie 4 ft of 2-lb hook length to the 3-lb main line, using the water knot. In the wind this can be a bit tricky, so it helps to practise at home. Four ft of line not only gives a long, natural fall but also ensures that later, if you move the tackle along the bottom, the bait will be at least 3 ft from the feeder. This can be an important factor when bream fishing, although less so with most other species.

The choice of bite indicator can be difficult. Conditions are nearly perfect for slack-lining, but there will certainly be some undertow as the wind has been blowing hard for some hours,

101

so unless you are experienced, you will be better off using a swingtip or quivertip. And, all round, the quivertip is the more versatile of the two, provided you can get a good angle between the tip and the line. So a quivertip it is – quite a light, sensitive one – and three rod rests go in to hold the rod steady. Sit with your back to the wind, as this is most comfortable, and no-one fishes well if they are uncomfortable.

The hook is a size 20 – a good all-round size that will take small roach and will also be capable of landing bream. The main requirement is that it should be forged, as hitting a bream at 30 yd in a strong wind will easily straighten a fine-wire hook unless you are very experienced in using this sort of tackle in these conditions. It should be a spade end whipped direct to the end. This is something else you can practise at home, and is essential for the leger angler to learn. If you buy only ready-whipped hooks you are stuck with the length and strength of nylon you are given. Whipping your own is not only quicker, but also cheaper and, most importantly, gives you complete freedon of choice of hook and line.

If you want to use a bigger bait like a worm, you will have to move up to a size 18 or a 16, or perhaps even a size 14. The 2-lb line will be quite sufficient to take these sizes, and is a good reason for starting off with a 2-lb hook length. If you start with, say, 1 lb, you are approaching danger level if you try to pull a size 16 into a fish at 30 yd, and using a size 14 to 1 lb line can easily result in a break. If you use a 2-lb hook length, you will be more likely to swop hook sizes when you need to.

In short, unless you are one of the small minority of anglers who will take the trouble to change your tackle as soon as it is necessary, you will need to take the middle road all though your fishing career. Using the 3-lb main line is a great compromise, as it will cover almost all the situations you are likely to come across in an ordinary day's fishing. The only alternative is to have two or three leger rods set up, all with different main lines and hook lengths.

Using the groundbait feeder

When you are ready to start fishing, you should check the groundbait again. Almost certainly you will need to add a little more water and give it another good mix. You will have to add water at intervals during the day to keep it at the right consistency. Conversely, you should also make sure that if it rains your groundbait is covered, as too much water is worse than not enough! A mist spray such as those sold at garden centres is absolutely invaluable for adding a tiny amount of

102

water, spread all over the bowl. If you work quickly you can get away with tipping some in, but this tends to wet the groundbait in one particular spot; a mist spray is much better. They are cheap as well, and probably as good value for money as any other accessory the leger angler will ever buy, because mixing groundbait to the wrong consistency is the worst mistake he can make (apart from smashing off when he strikes).

The next job is to bait the hook. You must always do this before filling the feeder, whatever type it is. If you don't, you will have to lay the feeder down for several seconds, during which time the maggots may start to break up the groundbait, especially if you have added a few pinkies, which are a very active maggot. Laying the tackle down also increases your chances of tangling the line in undergrowth. Use just a single hook maggot as bait, as this will take any size of fish which swims, and should at least bring a bite or two, which always gives the angler confidence.

Now is the time to fill the feeder, and you have a choice of adding either a load of squatts and casters to the bowl of groundbait, or just a few in one spot, mixing them in and filling the feeder from part of the bowl. This latter is the way all the books and experts tell you is best, but it is not easy. I favour putting lots of squatts in and adding just a few casters each time I fill the feeder, as these can dry out in the course of the day and become floaters, taking the fish out of your swim as they drift away. So put in the squatts, give a mix round, and add a few casters in one spot, just mixing them in with your finger. Using just one hand (usually your left if you are right-handed), push the feeder lengthways through the groundbait for 1–2 in and shovel the feed in with your thumb at one and and your fingers at the other, packing it in fairly hard. Finally, pinch both ends together to make sure it is firm.

If you are clever, you will now try a little experiment. Drop the feeder into the water close to the bank where you can see it. Drop it from a fair height, and see what the groundbait does. Odd little pieces may float out as it sinks, but the main bulk should stay in the feeder for several seconds at least, before it starts floating out. After 30 seconds jerk the feeder to see whether this leaves most of the feed on the bottom. If it does, the consistency is about right. If you have used one of the special feeder groundbaits, you may see a sort of 'explosion' as the feed inside absorbs more water and forces its way out through the holes, making a little cloud. If this happens congratulate yourself – you have got it dead right. You can try this experiment at home to check your mixing procedure. Indeed you should do so. Twenty minutes spent experimenting like this is worth a whole season of trial and error on the bankside.

103

Adding crushed hemp sets a stream of particles rising to the surface, and then falling, attracting fish.

Tactics

Bait the hook, re-fill the feeder and cast the rig out. Two to three feet of line between rod tip and swimfeeder is about right as you cast. Keep it nice and smooth, and stand if you find it easier. When the feeder hits the water feather the line with your forefinger to stop a big arc of line being blown out to one side by the wind, but don't click the bale arm shut. Put the rod tip down to surface level and watch as the tip is bent round by the sinking feeder. Then you will see the tip jerk back a little, and that is the time to shut the bale arm. As a very rough guide, an average leger weight or swimfeeder takes about one second to sink about 2 ft, according to how

104

tight the line is. The stronger the wind blows, the tighter the line tends to be.

Now is the time to take up the slack line and watch for a bite. However, you cannot do this properly until all the line has been sunk between rod tip and swimfeeder. Any line still lying on the surface will give all sorts of false indications as it is buffeted by the wind and waves. So plunge the rod under the surface as far as you can and reel in two or three turns very quickly. If you can see your line on the surface you will be able to see it cut through the water as you tighten up.

Groundbait exploding from a feeder attracts fish. If your hook length is 3 ft longer than the link to your swimfeeder (top), then pulling the rig (centre) will pull the bait nearer to the cloud. If you get it dead right and pull it exactly 3 ft (bottom), your bait should be lying with the other free offerings. After you've had several casts the fish should, of course, be hunting over a wider area, because you can't get every cast into the same spot. Note, that as the feeder moves it may also kick up little clouds of mud.

105

Experience will tell you when you have sunk all the line, and then you can begin to watch for any indications of fish. Tighten as described earlier, so there is a tiny bit of slack line at the end of the quivertip, which will be straight. The drift will take up the slack line and the tip will probably end up with the tiniest bit of a curve in it.

If, as is common, nothing happens in the first five minutes or so, it is time to start moving the bait in the hope of getting a take. And as a general rule you should start by giving just tiny twitches. The reason for this is that the feeder is a large object, and could possibly frighten finicky fish at this stage if it suddenly jumps a long way, so the less movement you can give it the better for the moment, and a twitch of only ½ in on the bait could be enough to induce a bite if a fish has its eye on it.

Twitching and searching

The exact process of twitching is described in Chapter 7, and you have a choice of several methods, all of which move the feeder and trail the bait along behind it. For your first cast with a feeder you should aim to pull the bait at least 4–5 ft in total, so it passes through the area of the lake bed you have groundbaited. It can do no harm, and if the groundbait has attracted small fish, as it often does, you may at least get a bite or two, which works wonders for your confidence. It also pulls the bait into view if it's hidden by a small piece of weed or rubbish on the bottom. The most likely scenario, however, is that you will have two or three casts in the first 30 minutes without seeing a bite. Console yourself with the thought that at least you are getting groundbait into your swim, and will hope to reap the rewards later.

It may be, however, that you get the feeling that the fish are some way away from your groundbaited area. Perhaps other anglers are catching on a different line. You won't have too much feed out there, and it shouldn't have done any damage. So it's worth searching the swim, but with a straight leger to begin with. If nearby anglers are catching fish it shows that the fish are in a feeding mood, and a straight leger could take one or two. If you use a swivel link to the feeder, you will be able to unclip it and slip on an Arlesey bomb. It takes only seconds, and you are free to cast anywhere you wish with less disturbance than when using the feeder, and without putting any groundbait in.

Camouflaging the feeder

Another great advantage of pulling a swimfeeder through the swim is that every time you move it, a little puff of mud will show. Without doubt this is attractive to all fish, and is a good reason for using a feeder. However, you still have to consider that a normal, shop-bought feeder with a silvery lead weight attached is going to flash unnaturally every time you move it. For this reason some anglers – usually the best matchmen – camouflage theirs by marking them all over with a black felt pen, and taking away the shine. This is easily done, on the bankside if necessary, and as the ink is spirit-based water will not wash it off. It's worth carrying a couple of black felt pens just to do this job.

Counting the retrieve

If you catch a fish it is essential that you know the direction and distance at which you caught it. So you should always make a habit of counting the number of turns of the reel handle when you retrieve, and especially when you hook a fish. Then you will know whether you are getting back into the same spot each time. And after a little experience you will be able to make a fair guess at how far you are casting. The technically minded among you can, in fact, work out the approximate distance at which you are fishing by checking the retrieve rate of the reel and working out a simple equation. The equation gives you the circumference of a circle: $2 \times pi \times r$, when r is the radius of the spool. Most modern match spools are about 2 in across, so the radius is 1 in. One squared is 1; and $2 \times pi = 6.284$, so one circle of the spool will retrieve about six inches. If the retrieve ratio is 4:1, you are retrieving about 2 ft of line per turn. The faster reels are nearer 5:1, which gives $2\frac{1}{2}$ ft per turn. So 30 turns will, on average, work out at around 20–25 yd.

Counting is essential on lakes and wide rivers such as the Welland, Huntspill, Thames, Witham or the Great Ouse Relief Channel. On these waters an error in re-casting of two to three turns (about 6 ft) is usually acceptable, provided you have the direction right. Use some sort of marker on the opposite bank to achieve this. However, it is also useful on narrower waters, when an error of no more than about 3 ft may be needed to get you bait plum into the right spot. Then, one turn too many or too little may be sufficient to warn you that you do not have the distance quite right.

If you are fishing in a match on a lake it's definitely worth checking, early on, how many turns your competitors are taking to retrieve. Even if you can't see their hands you can always tell each time they make a turn by the way the rod tip bobs up and down! And if they have a good fish on, make every effort to check the turns if you can. It is also useful to count the number of turns you make when playing a good fish, so you get some idea of how far away it is at any one time.

107

Above: Some top anglers camouflage their feeders.

Right: Small bream like this just love groundbait.

Finding the fish

There's an excellent chance, given that the conditions of a warm, strong wind are good for feeding fish, that you will get a bite or two as you search around the swim with the straight leger rig. If they are just small roach you may need only to remember the spot for exploring later and, having now given your groundbaited place a short rest, cast back into this swim with your leger tackle. If you don't get a bite it's worth considering whether you have the groundbait in the right place. Local knowledge, or advice from other anglers, should be what you rely on most. And if you decide to groundbait another area you should make a mental note of how many turns it takes to retrieve your tackle from the original baited swim, for it's likely you will want to go back to it at intervals during the day.

108

A good tip is to slip a rubber band on to the spool when you think you have gone just a yard or two past the right spot. Then when you cast you can pull line off until the band is reached and reel in, say, five turns. If the line is then tight, you have it dead right. The books tell you to put the band on when you have it dead right, but I doubt whether the authors have ever actually done this – you need a few turns extra to allow for error. Alternatively you can slip the line under the little clip that is provided on some models for holding the line when you pack up. Or a dab of typist's correction fluid on the line can mark the required spot.

Bites in these warm, windy conditions are likely to be good, with fish putting a real bend in the quivertip. And you should be certain to set the clutch so it gives, and clicks, when you hit a fish, as in a strong wind it can sometimes be difficult to be sure whether you have a fish on, especially when using a swimfeeder. Watch the rod tip carefully so you can tell how much pressure you are putting on and where the fish is running. If you get good fish, stick with the groundbait feeder if everything works out all right, and if you want to introduce more feed do so using a bigger feeder. Remember that it will now weigh more, so you should consider changing to a 4-lb line. The 3-lb line is, however, a good all-round strength for this sort of fishing, and will comfortably cast up to ¾ oz or more provided the cast is smooth. There's no reason why you shouldn't introduce balls of groundbait by hand at any time, but only if you are certain you can get them into exactly the right position. At 30-yd range you can do a lot of damage by spreading the groundbait around, so you may put out six balls and get only one dead on target. Generally a feeder is the best bet at this range unless you have experience of adding groundbait balls. At worst, if you miscast a swimfeeder you put some feed outside your swim; at best it feeds your swim at the same rate at which you are getting bites – more bites, more feed; fewer bites, less feed.

The groundbait feeder is quite versatile, and if you want to put worms into the swim plug one end with groundbait, put the chopped worms in the middle, and plug the other end. Be sure to press firmly; don't risk the lot blowing apart as you cast. You may need to add just a little extra water for this job; it doesn't matter how the groundbait behaves, so long as it eventually discharges its contents. The main aim is to get the worms into your swim. In fact, without doubt this is the best method of all of getting worms into any swim. Even if you have been feeding groundbait by hand, it's worth putting on a groundbait feeder for that specific purpose, as they tend to break groundbait up.

Later in the day you may want to use a block-end feeder, which will allow you to put in maggots without groundbait.

On the whole, in the conditions we have described there will be no advantage in doing this, as small roach, gudgeon and bream of all sizes love groundbait, and it's mainly in cold, difficult conditions that maggots on their own may bring more bites.

If you do get into a shoal of bream there's a very good argument for swopping the groundbait feeder for a straight leger, as a feeder dragged through the swim can disturb the bream. Worse, if you hook a fish the feeder is hanging from the line and is more likely to whack a fish than is a straight leger, because it's many times larger. In Ireland, where the bream shoals tend to be bigger than in England, and where they get less attention from the angler, this is not a consideration. In England, especially on waters that are match-fished, the fish almost always become finicky after a time, and it may mean the difference between getting four or five fish and going on to land a dozen or more.

With carp or roach, swopping to a leger weight will probably not be necessary, as the fish in the shoal soon recover from any fright. In fact, with carp in particular you may find that you play the fish for so long that while you are doing so the rest mop up all the groundbait you've put out. So a change to a larger feeder may be called for simply to get plenty of feed into the swim again.

Frame feeders

Though different from other feeders, the frame feeder is most closely aligned with the open-ended feeder. You can't put bait inside it, so you squeeze groundbait around the feeder. This means that it has to be just a little bit more 'sticky' than that used in most groundbait feeders, both to hold together while being cast, and to avoid it breaking up too soon when it hits the water, if this is what you require. A little extra water added to the mixture will help achieve this, as will looking round for a proprietory groundbait that has a good binding property. A frame feeder tends to be just a little quicker to use than filling a normal feeder, but you have to be doubly careful that the contents don't break up when you cast – so squatts and casters are much better than pinkies and hook maggots. You can also use sweetcorn in the groundbait.

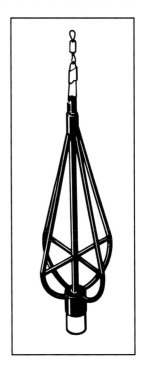

The strange-looking Thamesley frame feeder – groundbait is squeezed around it, but it works well.

111

CHAPTER TEN

BLOCK-END FEEDERS

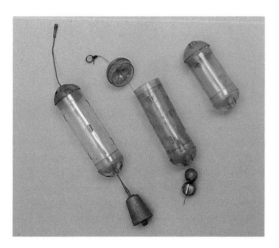

Above left: the Feederlink is a versatile feeder. Use it with the link provided (left); or on a nylon link with shot (centre); or you can cut it in half, replace the cap, and use it when you need only a few maggots inside (right).

Above right: for fast water, block-end feeders may need extra weight added. Special weights are sold for this purpose. In fast water you may have to glue a big ski weight on. This one (right) has also been wired on for extra security.

These are rather more versatile swimfeeders than the open-ended type, as they can be used easily on all types of water, from those that are completely still, like canals, to fast-moving rivers like the Severn or the Upper Trent.

Both ends have a cap, one of which must be capable of being removed so the feeder can be filled with maggots and replaced. It is important to make sure that this cap is attached to the line in some way so that it cannot be lost if it happens to work loose. Baits other than maggots can, theoretically, be used inside, but on a stillwater maggots are the obvious choice, as they will wriggle out through the holes along the sides and in the caps. On a faster water the current may be sufficient to force the bait out, and casters and hemp are often used either with, or instead of, maggots.

Several different models are on the market, and there is no real alternative to trying them to see which suits you best. The Drennan Feederlink is particularly useful, because it can be easily cut down, and used with about a dozen maggots on winter days when the fish are finicky. This is a small, light feeder and would be used only on still or very slow-moving waters. On fast rivers the choice is very important, because

A simple set-up, with the feeder running on a length of nylon between two swivels.

the feeder must be strong enough to withstand constant casting and – even more important – constant filling. Unfortunately the action of repeatedly taking off the cap and replacing it, perhaps once a minute for five hours, always finds the weak spot if there is one. So until you settle on a particular model you will have to resign yourself to carrying several spares if you are going to fish one of these fast rivers that requires constant feeding. I find the feeders with screw-on caps the strongest all-round, but it's easy to spend several seconds getting the cap screwed on properly, which is frustrating when the fish are feeding well. All may, at some time, need extra weight attached to them, because the secret of fast-water fishing with a swimfeeder is to get the weight absolutely right.

You will find that when several ounces of lead have been added, as may be necessary in really fast swims, the feeder itself is liable to disintegrate because of the extra strain it undergoes during casting, hitting the water and trundling along the bottom. Special ski-leads, which look like a couple of parallel skis, are sold for swimfeeders that need large amounts of weight added. The intended method of

113

attachment is with short lengths of lead sold specially for the purpose, or with short spikes incorporated in the main weight, which go through the holes in the side of the swimfeeder. However, these tend to tear the feeder apart after a time. I have never found a better method of attaching ski leads, or similar large weights, than glueing them to the side with Araldite. This is a tip given to me by matchman Tom Bedder. And as an extra precaution I wire them on, as the Araldite can come away from the feeder after a few outings.

Rigs

The same type of paternoster as that used with a straight leger is probably the most popular set-up. And for stillwater fishing, or on slowly moving rivers, this is usually fine, allowing the bait to be fished 'on the drop' with a tail of up to 5 ft. However, for fishing fast water there are several points to be looked at, and two main methods of attachment, – paternoster-style, or with the line running through the feeder in exactly the same way as through a drilled bullet – both of which will work very well at different times.

On fast water the length of drop rarely needs to be longer than 2 ft or so, and often it is much shorter. The main problems are technical ones: making sure that the tackle is adequate, that the line doesn't twist round the link joining the feeder to the main line, and developing a routine so that as little time as possible is lost when the fish are feeding. It's useful to cover the two different types of water on which a block-end feeder is used, by fishing two imaginary swims. Wherever you use a block-end feeder, you are likely to need to adapt one of these techniques.

STILLWATER FISHING

Venue – very slowly moving river
Depth – 5 ft
Current – left to right
Wind – none
Sun – bright
Season – winter

These are conditions in which fish are likely to be very finicky, so a very cautious approach is called for – not only in the way you physically move up to the water, but also in the way you tackle the fish. The first point to make is a very important one that applies to almost all situations in which you will use a swimfeeder. You should use the minimum amount of weight that will allow you to cast to your chosen

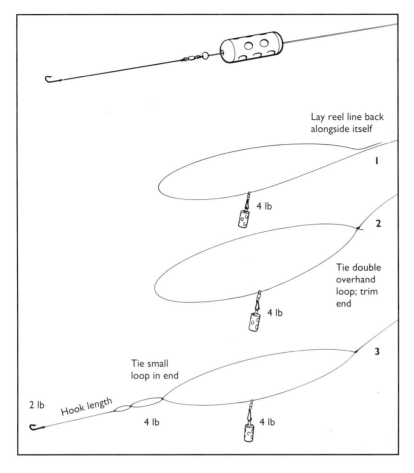

Lay reel line back
alongside itself

1

4 lb

2

Tie double
overhand
loop; trim
end

4 lb

3

Tie small
loop in end

2 lb

Hook length

4 lb

4 lb

Two easy block-end feeder rigs.
Top: the line runs through the feeder, stopped by a bead.
Bottom, 1: The line goes through the swivel and a loop is formed.
2: The loop is tied in a double overhand knot.
3: A small loop is tied in the end of the large loop. This is used to attach a hook length using the Two-loop method.

spot, provided this will also allow the feeder to just hold bottom. Although there is a slight movement here, the basic tactics will apply equally to a stillwater in winter, when the amount of wind and the distance you are casting will govern the amount of weight you use.

The Feederlink

With little or no movement on the water and no wind to inhibit casting it's likely that you will be able to use a tiny amount of weight – perhaps just a couple of swan shot. This is where the Feederlink comes into its own. It's a block-end feeder, but small and light with a nylon link running through the centre, and a weight attached to the end of the link. If this weight is too large, take out the link, thread your reel line through the centre of the caps so the line runs down the centre of the feeder when it is assembled, and pinch two swan shot on the end to hold the feeder on to the end of the line. This will provide all the weight you need for casting, and gives the extra advantage that if the feeder happens to

115

become snagged when you have a fish on, constant pressure will pull the shots off the line, leaving the feeder behind, but at least you will still get the fish. It's also extremely easy to add or to subtract weight using this method, and you will be much more inclined to do so than if you were using a feeder with an integral weight – so your catches should increase.

There is no point in using a sliding swivel set-up with a light feeder such as this – everything must be kept as delicate as possible. So with the Feederlink tied to the end of the reel line the hook length can be attached using the same water knot as that used on a straight leger rig, or by tying a loop about 6 in above the Feederlink and looping the hook length to this. The water is cold and the sun bright, which both point to fish feeding not very actively (if at all) and only on the bottom. So there is no need today to set up a 'long tail'. The Feederlink is, though, a good tool to use if you want to present a slow-sinking bait, as it is light and will itself sink fairly slowly. In summer when fishing at short range you can do worse than to use no weight at all on a Feederlink, just filling it with maggots to give it weight for casting and allowing the bait to sink slowly among the falling maggots. Today, choose an 18-in tail, which can be shortened if necessary, while the Feederlink is on a 6-in link. This set-up ensures that when the bait is in the water it is within 12 in or so of the feeder, and with fish perhaps unwilling to move many inches to pick up a bait it should pay dividends when they arrive in the swim. Two swan shot added to the feeder as described will be sufficient weight for casting, allowing the feeder to hold bottom but to be easily moved when necessary.

With no wind the choice of rod is not particularly important unless bankside vegetation dictates that you use a short one. However, it does mean you can use a very light quivertip to see the most delicate of bites. If there is no movement at all, slacklining would also work.

Feederlinks are small, which is fine for the conditions in this swim, when not much feed will be needed. Should you ever need to put out a larger amount of bait you can always adapt another feeder by attaching it in the same way. However, you will find good anglers reluctant to use large block-end feeders on stillwaters. If the fish are feeding well enough to warrant using a lot of feed the open-ended feeder is the usual choice, as this gets rid of the groundbait and maggots more quickly than a block-end. You should always try to ensure that your feeder is empty by the time you retrieve, otherwise you will be spreading the bait over a much greater area than you may think. So the medium-sized or large block-end is usually used only where there is a definite current to push the maggots through the holes.

Opposite: In cold weather, on canals or shallow waters, a cautious approach is called for.

117

Put simply, if you fill a medium-sized feeder with maggots it could take them five to ten minutes, or even more, to all crawl through the holes on a stillwater. And if you're waiting that long for a bite you probably don't need as much bait as that anyway. As with all groundbaiting you can add more later, but you can't take it out once it's in the swim.

Rod position

The river here is narrow – about as wide as the average canal – and because the sun is bright, and the fish will be easily spooked, you want to fish from as far away as possible. Start by casting downstream, to the right, about 15 yd away, and into the deepest water right in the middle of the river, which is only about 10 yd from your bank. While the general rule is that the rod is placed parallel to the bank when you are quivertipping, the conditions today suggest that you will be better off putting your rod straight out in front of you with the line streaming away to the right, but still forming a rough right-angle with the rod tip. You will find it easier to fish like this, as there is virtually no sideways pressure on the line from any current or wind. It would be perfectly all right to use a swingtip, but for most anglers it's easier to spot the tiny little nudges and quivers, that you are likely to get in these cool, bright conditions, on a quivertip.

Casting downstream

You should almost always cast downstream if the water is moving slowly, as the current drifts the maggots in the feeder down and away from you. This ensures that the fish in a feeding shoal are working their way towards you, and they see your bait before they come across the feeder or see the line (fish almost always feed by keeping their heads into the current and working their way upstream). If you were to cast upstream to your left, you would encourage the fish to travel under your rod, past your reel line, and up to the feeder to find the source of food, with the result that you will almost certainly scare them in these clear, bright conditions when you strike, if they have not already been frightened by seeing the line.

Try to guess where the depressions are – on the outside of bends, wherever the flow is fastest, and opposite tributaries or culverts are obvious choices. Alternatively you can plumb the depth with a float, but you must take care to do it as quietly as possible on a cool day like this when fish may be timid. If you do this, then often a pole is the perfect answer – you can drop the plummet in, and lift it out, with very little disturbance. A good tip is to use a big plummet, as it is easy to tell when it has hit the bottom.

Line twist

A single maggot on the hook is the obvious choice, and a pinkie is a good one to start with. A single maggot, of whatever type, helps prevent line twist, which can happen when you are using two maggots, and which is the bane of the leger angler's life. The line is less likely to twist if you retrieve slowly; or you can put the hook through the whole length of one maggot and nick a second one just on the point. After many years wrestling with the problem of line twist, which is especially bad if you use a hook length of less than 1 lb, I have plumped for using just one maggot on the hook as my usual solution.

If your hook length does twist, you must change it, because it has been weakened, and will only twist again and again, even doing so as the bait sinks, not just on the retrieve. It's a real bind in cold weather, so try to avoid it at all costs. I have found that ½-lb line is much less liable to twist than the lower strengths, but on a day like today you must aim simply to get a bite or two to give you confidence, and that will mean starting with a size 24 to a 12-oz bottom and a single pinkie. If that does not bring bites, change to a single squatt, which is even smaller.

Just one point about a size 24 on 12-oz nylon. You would be well advised to buy such hooks ready tied unless you have a hook tier and are extremely confident that you can whip the hook on without kinking the light nylon. I have whipped hooks on by hand, on the bank, for 35 years. However, I would not attempt to do so with 12-oz nylon as it is so delicate, and I leave a kink of some sort on two occasions out of three, which means I have to re-whip it – a time-consuming business even when the hands are warm, and next-to-impossible in cold weather.

A typical day

Let's start fishing. Bait the hook with a single pinkie, then fill the feeder, ensuring that the cap is firmly replaced. Cast immediately, otherwise the maggots in the feeder may start falling out. If the holes are too large you will know immediately, as you will see pinkies falling out as you cast. In that case some strips of electrician's tape wound round the feeder in a spiral will make the holes smaller. You make the first cast 15 yd downstream, and after five minutes and three or four little twitches, you haven't had a bite. Repeat this routine, but casting 1 ft closer each time.

Thirty minutes go by, and you've made six casts and haven't had a bite. It's worth trying a couple of yards further

119

out; cast, tighten the line just a little (in this shallow water there's not a lot of slack line anyway), and put the rod on the rest, allowing the very light flow to take up the remaining slack. Suddenly there's the tiniest of nudges on the tip – hardly enough to strike at. Retrieve and examine the pinkie. At first sight it looks untouched; but if you look very closely you can see it has been mouthed, as the skin is slightly scratched – there's no other way to describe it. It looks rough when compared with a pinkie from the bait box. It's important to look very hard at the bait after every single cast on a day like this, otherwise you can easily miss these markings. And to re-use that maggot will be a waste of time as you will probably never get a bite on it. You can tell by the fact that the skin is scratched well up the maggot that the fish has had it in its mouth, which is a good sign, showing that they are willing to feed properly, although they may have to be enticed.

The other main damage you'll often find on a maggot is that the tail has been sucked. You can clearly see when a fish has just marked the very tip. This indicates either a very small fish having a go, or that the fish are very finicky indeed and is, on the whole, a bad sign, suggesting that you may struggle to catch anything. If there are bream in the water the pinkie may just look limp. It's not easy for an inexperienced angler to spot this, but the maggot looks soft and stretched, although it may recover within a few seconds. Don't worry too much about checking this today, as the cold water can also make the maggot stretch and go lifeless.

This is the time to put a squatt on the hook, though for the moment keep filling the feeder with pinkies, as it's better to get them feeding on the larger-sized maggots if you can. The squatt is only half as big as the pinkie, and the size 24 hook is about right for it, anything much larger will look conspicuous. Re-cast and start concentrating – just one bite can set the adrenalin flowing. At least you know that there's something out there. And it's worth laying your hand very lightly on the rod handle ready to strike, being careful not to move the rod or you may get false indications. Even your heart thumping can transmit itself to a sensitive quivertip on a calm day like this.

After only 10 seconds there's a definite movement of about $\frac{1}{2}$ in on the quivertip and you've struck instinctively. It's not a big fish, but remember that you've only a 12-oz hook length, so take it easy. It's a roach of about 2 oz, which you can just about lift out. Anything larger will need the landing net as the hook length is so fragile. Better to net all small fish than have one wriggle, as you swing it in, and break the very delicate nylon.

The 10-second delay between casting and getting a bite shows that the fish probably took the bait before it hit the bottom. The hook is only a fine-wire model, and very small, so with the maggot on it sinks slowly. If you should move up to a size 20 forged hook it will sink very much faster. You should bear this sink-rate in mind when fishing with small baits like a single squatt or a single pinkie. Anyway, if you get two or three bites quickly it will be worth lengthening the drop from 18 in to 3 ft, in case the fish come up in the water.

Out the line goes again, and again you've got a roach. There must be something in this spot that's holding the shoal, so try to pinpoint it. In this case it's right on the point of the reflection of a bush growing on the far bank, and in a direct line between you and a church spire in the distance. Pole anglers don't have this problem because their pole and fixed-length line ensure that they get the bait into the same spot each time.

It's worth putting a pinkie on again, to see whether the fish will take a bait this big, especially as you have kept using pinkies in the feeder. So out the tackle goes again, and you wait for a bite. Sure enough the tip moves just that ½ in and again you've got a fish on. This is a small bream of about 3 oz, which fights quite well on this delicate tackle and should certainly be netted.

Bites

As with all legering, you will often find that the small, definite movements of the quivertip or swingtip produce a much higher percentage of successful strikes than the days when fish take the tip right round. This probably happens because when the fish are feeding well, they are taking the bait casually, and, feeling quite secure they stay where they are, looking for more feed. So the movement at the tip is minimal. On the days when the tip really cracks round, this could be due to the fish being nervous about feeding, but suddenly making up their minds to take the bait, and going screaming off with it as if they are half-expecting a problem. It's noticeable on heavily fished carp waters that lots of bites nearly take the rod out of your hand. Whatever the reason, today has produced three fish from four bites, so far, and all have been slight, but confident.

Changing conditions on stillwaters

It's now about 10 o'clock in the morning, and a slight breeze is springing up. This happens on perhaps three out of four calm days, and is almost always a good sign, provided the wind is not too cold. On waters up to 5–6 ft deep, you can now expect the fish to feed with much more confidence, as the ripple on the water makes movement on the bank less

121

obvious. And even on deeper waters – up to 15–20 ft deep – that ripple definitely makes a difference. Also, cloud is now covering the sun, which is an excellent sign as nine times out of ten sport is better on an overcast day than in bright sunlight.

The next cast has produced another small bream – a good sign, as bream tend not to roam about quite as much as roach, though they are both shoal fish. And now, with the ripple and cloud cover, the next fish is about 6 oz. As things look like hotting up a bit, it would be wise to change the hook length for something stronger. If you are experienced you could try a size 22 hook to 1 lb; if you do not feel confident about playing reasonable fish on this tackle, you could use a size 20 to 1½ lb nylon.

A change to the 20 hook means re-tackling completely by cutting the reel line above the water knot, tying the hook length on via a water knot, 9 in above the feeder, and then re-tying the Feederlink to the end of the reel line. It would be wise to allow a 3-ft hook length to give a longer drop. Then the spade end hook is whipped direct to the hook length. The beauty of this system is that you can use any combination of nylon and hook size. And if you can't whip the hook on by hand on the bank, buy a hook-whipping machine. They cost only £1–£2 and are worth their weight in gold, saving you their cost many times over if you are used to buying ready-whipped hooks. The disadvantage of this water knot system lies in the time it takes to re-tie it – probably only a couple of minutes, but it can seem like a lifetime when the fish are feeding.

With a 3-ft drop on the bait you now have a chance of picking up more fish. However, if things should get hard and you think you are getting bites you can't see reduce it back to 18 in. If that doesn't work, go back to the size 24 hook on a 12-oz bottom. However, the cautious start has paid dividends, and on a winter's day like this you can expect fish to feed on and off until about 2 pm or slightly later. When you suddenly feel the temperature drop, that's the time to be prepared to go home, for the fish are likely to stop feeding altogether.

MOVING WATER

Venue – fast-moving river
Depth – 6 ft
Current – left to right
Wind – strong downstream
Sun – bright
Season – summer

The first objective in this swim is to get a fairly constant stream of bait out to at least the centre of the river some 20 yd away. Loose-fed maggots will probably be swept away in seconds, before they have had time to sink; and an open-ended feeder could have its contents washed out very quickly before even it hits the bottom. Heavy cereal groundbait might work, but you will have to make it very stiff indeed, which is not easy, and groundbaiting like that gives you no chance to search the river. You would have to put several very big balls into one spot and take a chance on that spot holding fish. The answer is a block-end feeder, which will be baiting the swim with 40 to 50 maggots every time you cast out. In addition you can use a heavy feeder, with at least 2 oz on it, so it gets to the bottom immediately and stays there, releasing its contents slowly. Use hook maggots, as they are heavier than pinkies or squatts, and will not be swept away quite so quickly. In any case you need to use a fair-sized hook because you are after chub and barbel from 6 oz up to 4 lb or even more.

Tackle

With a feeder weighing 2 oz you must use a proper feeder rod. An ordinary light quivertip will not have enough power to cast a heavy weight, nor to retrieve it, nor to play a big fish in this type of water. The exact make is not important, but you should be prepared to pay a fair amount for a powerful rod to do the job properly. If you don't have a feeder rod, a carp rod will do quite well.

The line will need to be around 5 lb or more, to cope with the strain of continual casting and retrieving as well as the bumps it will receive as it rolls down the swim and possibly into snags. I have a reel with 8-lb line on it, and there is no danger of the line breaking if I happen to miscast. However, it does mean that if I want to go down to a 2½-lb hook length the tackle tends to be unbalanced. If you are going to fish fast rivers where there are big barbel you should certainly have some 6-lb or 8-lb line with you, because one day you're going to need it.

The reel should be strong, though you'll get away with your normal match reel with a bit of luck. If you are going to fish a water like this consistently, you should get a big, strong reel – the sort used by specimen hunters, as the continual hard use will eventually ruin a delicate match reel. It should not be automatic – the weight of the big feeder on the line will certainly affect the automatic spring system. If you have to use an automatic (and I have, in the past), be sure to open the bale arm by flicking the arm and hold the line with your finger when you cast.

123

Look for obstructions in fast water, as these tend to hold chub and barbel.

The rod rest is very important. The line is so strong and thick that the current has a far greater effect on it than on the thin lines used for stillwater angling. To reduce this pull, it's usual to hold the rod high so as little line as possible is in the water. Unfortunately these fast rivers almost invariably have rocky bottoms into which it is difficult to push a rod rest. I use a sea angling tripod, which is absolutely perfect as it can be positioned anywhere in a second or two. The best alternative is the commercially produced rest, which has to be pushed into the bottom but which has a swivelling arm to hold the end of the butt at elbow level. This means that the rod tip is very high indeed. If you haven't got this, you'll have to use two normal rests – one high and one low.

On waters which hold big chub and barbel the hook must be forged. You can still go down to a size 20 if you wish, but a fine-wire hook is asking for trouble. You'll stand a better chance of hooking a fish on a forged size 20 than on a fine-wire 14, which will almost certainly straighten when you hook a decent fish.

The feeder

For simplicity, use a Mal Storey Feeder, which has a large strip of lead down the side, with the ends bent round the edges of the body. The cap on the bottom is stapled to the body, while the cap at the top is removable. This has a long slit in it,

A modern rod rest made especially for swimfeeder anglers.

through which a loop of line will go if you want to use it paternoster-style. This loop is then fixed to the main reel line via a sliding swivel. The other end of the loop is attached to the feeder by looping it under the strip of lead.

The alternative method of fixing the feeder is rather easier, and becoming quite popular among anglers who regularly fish these fast rivers for chub and barbel. The line goes through the centre of the feeder, and is prevented from hitting the bait by a bead. This, in turn, is stopped either by the knot joining the hook length, or by a swivel. Easiest of all is to carry the feeder already threaded on to an 18-in length of nylon with a tiny swivel at either end, and a small bead at the bottom so the swivel does not jam into the feeder. Just tie the top swivel to your reel line, and tie the hook length to the bottom swivel. Then you are ready to start fishing. You will find, when you first fish fast water like this, that simplicity is the key to catching fish, and if the feeder happens to become damaged it takes only seconds to tie on another. This system also does away almost completely with tangles.

125

The paternoster method involves having about 4 in of line from the feeder to a swivel, through which the reel line runs, also stopped by a bead. To prevent tangles you can cover this link with rubber tubing. The great advantage of this method is that should the feeder become jammed in rocks or a snag the fish can still be played. The line runs through the swivel, and there's an excellent chance of the fish pulling the feeder free. A Power Gum link is also available. This cushions the strike, and you should certainly carry some. Apart from being ready to use, they work very well, allowing you to hit the fish, when you strike, before you move the feeder. And they could considerably increase your hooking rate.

As to the make of feeder, this is a matter of personal preference, and it largely depends on the type of river you fish. The solid green feeders are very strong indeed and are deservedly popular, while there are also flat feeders, which theoretically hold bottom better. These are nice in snaggy water where you need to cast to a spot and hold the feeder there. The round ones, particularly those that have a groove down the side to take a strip of lead, are good if you want to search a water by rolling the feeder along the swim in the flow. You must realise that lead attached to the outside of the feeder will always inhibit the rolling effect. Some feeders have a compartment inside in which you can insert extra weight. These are a delight to use, although just a little bit fiddly. On most feeders there is a weak spot somewhere that will cause them to break after prolonged, hard use. Sometimes this is the body, or it could be the point of attachment. You must be prepared, therefore, with some spare feeders in your box. And you must also have some small, add-on weights. These come in two or three shapes. I like the simple $\frac{1}{4}$ oz strips, each end of which is inserted through a hole and bent round inside to hold it. These small weights are the key to success with this type of fishing.

Today you can use the simple set-up with the line running direct through the feeder, which holds 2 oz of weight, and a forged size 14 to 2 ft of 3-lb line tied to the bottom swivel.

Filling the feeder

As with the Feederlink, it's important to bait the hook first and then fill the feeder and cast straight away. The size of the holes can be very important on this fast-running water. If the feeder seems to be releasing the bait too fast, the strip of electrician's tape partly blocking the holes will work; but if, as can happen when the fish are feeding well, you are getting a bite before the feeder is completely empty, the holes should be enlarged. The pliable plastic type can be easily cut with a pair of scissors. It's important not to be playing a fish with maggots still pouring from the feeder, as this disperses your bait instead of concentrating it in one spot.

An apron is essential on this type of water, as it's often necessary to stand in the margins. A pint or two of maggots is put in the front of the apron, and it saves an enormous amount of time. Just pull the feeder over the apron pocket and as you scoop maggots in it doesn't matter if they fall out – they just end back in the apron. Start with three hook maggots from the same pocket, as bait.

It's difficult to know where to start fishing if you have no local knowledge. However, the fish tend to stay within 1 to 2 ft of features on the bottom, and these will often be given away by swirls on the surface. The snag itself will be above the spot where the swirls start, and perhaps a few feet upstream. If there are no obvious features, start by casting just upstream. This way the maggots will not end up too far downstream. If you were to cast well downstream, the maggots could finish up 40 yd below you, and you would have no hope of trundling the feeder down to the shoal. This goes against the advice given for fishing a slowly moving water, but in a fact water the fish are likely to be much more active, ignoring the line in their eagerness to get at the bait. And getting the shoal feeding is your first priority.

Bait the size 14 forged hook with three maggots, fill the feeder, replace the cap, and cast out just upstream, to your left. The cast is more of a swing than a whiplash cast such as you might give a light leger lead, and now you can see why you need a proper swimfeeder rod. Two ounces doesn't sound much to cast, but in fact it's a very heavy weight. Don't tighten the line – leave the bow – the current will tighten this up in just a few seconds.

The bow

The secret to fast-water swimfeeder fishing is the bow in the line, which should be quite big. And the bigger the bow, the

**1: In fast running water you should allow a bow to form in the line.
2: A fish will normally approach the bait from downstream.
3: It will continue upstream until the line to the swimfeeder is tight and it starts to move.
4: If you have the weight exactly correct, the moment the fish dislodges the swimfeeder it will be swept downstream and will hook the fish itself. This registers on the rod as a slack-line bite.**

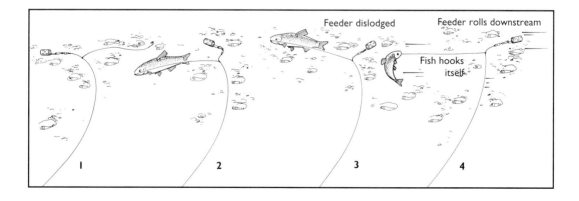

Feeder dislodged   Feeder rolls downstream

Fish hooks itself

1   2   3   4

Always bait your hook before filling the feeder, as maggots will soon crawl out of the holes.

lighter feeder you will be able to use to hold bottom. If you have the weight of the feeder correct, a fish taking the bait will dislodge the feeder, which will hurtle downstream, pulled by the bow. This will pull the hook into the mouth of the fish. And that's all there is to it! You would not believe the number of anglers who make things difficult for themselves by ignoring this simple procedure. Of course, there are days when it doesn't work out quite right, or the fish are feeding too cautiously. But you must get the basics right before you start adapting them. It's exactly the same principle as beach anglers use; and it's probably the biggest single fault most of them make – they don't get the bow big enough.

In a match, it's against the rules to cast upstream, of course. Even so, many clubs will allow you to pinch the odd yard in this fast water, and since everybody is fishing the same way there's no problem. It definitely helps improve catches. Today you are not in a match, so it's upstream, and the feeder is swept by the current downstream, to rest a few feet to your right. Leave the bow in the line where it is, put the rod on the rest and watch the rod tip.

The first priority on a water like this is to get plenty of maggots into the swim. After about 45 seconds retrieve the tackle and repeat the exercise, checking that no maggots are left in the feeder. When you first wind the feeder back against a fast current you'll probably think you've got a fish on – everybody does. However, after a few casts you get to know how much resistance the current puts up. When you get a fish on, you'll be left in no possible doubt!

Ten casts later, without a bite, and it's time to leave this one a bit longer. Three minutes go by and there's still no

A 12-oz chub will put up a good fight in stream water.

response. Now pick the rod up and ease it upwards slowly, watching the line tighten. Suddenly, as the feeder starts rolling downstream, the line will slacken. Now just put the rod back on the rest. Did you see that? As you put the rod down the tip started jerking violently back and forth. The movement of the bait obviously tempted a fish to take it, and it dislodged the feeder again. The bite is not that described in text books ('...suddenly the rod tip slammed down'), but a real dance. Pick the rod up. There, you have a fish on. Hooked by itself. And it's really bending the rod over. You have 5-lb line on, with a 3-lb bottom, so you can afford to give the fish some wellie. It takes a few fish to get used to the tackle, and you'll be amazed at how the current magnifies the power of the fish.

Now the fish goes across the current, and you're keeping the rod high, which is good. Lowering it only gives the current more line to push against, helping the fish and increasing your arm strain. Try to get the fish into the side, where the water is slacker. It's been on two or three minutes and it's in the side, about 15 yd downstream. You'll need a bit

129

of patience now, bringing it up against the moderate flow. It's a chub, and when it opens its mouth the current almost sweeps it downstream again. Bring the fish in close – it is a slow process. You'll find that you need to bring it well over the net. You can't lean forward to push the net that extra foot out because as you do so the current takes the fish downstream and out of range. So bring it well upstream, and don't lift the net until the fish is completely over the rim, remembering that as soon as you release pressure, even slightly, the fish will sweep downtream again.

Now you can examine your prize. The fish you thought was at least 3 lb turns out to be about 12 oz! You have to experience this type of fishing before you can truly believe it. Incidentally, if the feeder runs directly along the reel line you have a small advantage when you land fish; the feeder appears above the surface of the water earlier than it would if it were on a paternoster link, and this reduces the current pressure. It's a small point, but a good reason for choosing this method for your first trip or two.

Holding the rod

It's impossible to beat holding the rod all day. You can feel weed catching the line, the feeder bumping over stones, and even fish mouthing the bait – something you can't see on the rod tip. This creates a sort of rasping feeling, as if someone was sawing through the line. You also get to distinguish gudgeon bites from 'proper' bites given by better fish. Best of all, you can move the feeder just the smallest amount and be prepared for a bite a few seconds later. Many times you will find yourself playing fish without remembering how you struck – it's an instinctive reaction. On a snaggy water, if you are holding the rod, you also have that second of extra time to hold the fish away from its safe haven, for a big barbel will often be almost in a snag when it takes the bait. It's not unusual for even the best anglers to have days when almost every fish seems to get snagged. Whether they come out is in the lap of the gods. All you can do is to keep a tight line for as long as you think you have a chance of getting the fish, or give it slack line when you're desperate.

Tactics

As a general rule, fish will feed in quite a small area of the river – perhaps in a depression, or near a bed of weed or a rock. And as long as you keep catching fish you should continue to cast to the same spot, and fish the same way. At some time, though, bites will dry up, and then it's time to alter tactics. When the fish are feeding, a drop down to a smaller feeder, which is quicker to fill and easier to cast can pay dividends. You can go back to the big feeder, containing more maggots, if the fish go off the feed. Alternatively, they may have moved to another spot, and you should start searching the whole length of your swim, rolling the feeder down as far as you can. Often the fish will have holed up in a spot downstream and be waiting for the next lot of maggots to float by. If that doesn't work, try casting close to the far bank, or close to your own bank.

There are plenty of times, however, when you get the feeling that the fish are still there but not taking the bait properly. Perhaps you are getting half-hearted bites, and still hooking the odd fish. Then you should consider changing down to a size 20 hook with a single maggot; the hook must be forged, though. You might also want to drop the hook length down to 2 lb, or perhaps even 1½ lb if you are really desperate. Before you do that, however, you should consider changing the weight on the feeder. Try increasing the weight first (it's easier that way) by adding the small strips of lead available from many tackle shops, or by inserting weight in the little compartment provided on some models. An increase in weight help you to fish more accurately, although it will mean it's not so easy to twitch the bait.

More likely is that you should lighten the weight, and put a bigger bow in the line to hold it on the bottom. At least 50 per cent of the times when I have had fish go off in this fast water, lightening the feeder has put me in touch with the fish again.

Changing conditions on moving water

On most fast rivers, the flow can alter quite surprisingly during the day, and it's easy to carry on fishing without realising that the current is now only half the speed compared to half an hour ago. So keep an eye on the water level. It's a good idea to put a bank stick on the edge of the water, or to note the water level against the bank, so you get some idea of whether more water is coming down. If the level drops, it's odds-on that the current is slackening, and if it comes up it's likely the flow has increased. A change in current speed can also change the character of the swim, and may push the fish from one spot to another as the flow takes different courses. Unfortunately, an increase in flow often means that cold water is coming down the river, and this can put fish off the feed. Luckily on fast waters the fish are used to temperature changes, so they're likely to return to feeding as soon as the flow eases. This also applies to the slower-moving rivers, although here you are much more likely to notice a change in flow speed.

131

Holding the rod enables you to feel little knocks you won't see if you leave the rod to fish for itself.

Keep nets

You'll need to pay special attention to the position of the keep net in this type of fast water. The first priority is to make it stable, and this may mean using two or three bank sticks. Also, you must have it pointing downstream, and not across the current, because fish in the net will face into the current, and a big fish is unable to do this if the net is across the current. Also, it may not be able to move round. Correctly positioned, the net will allow the fish to line up behind each other. Be warned, though, that chub have a habit of launching themselves out of the mouth of the net, so place it well above the surface. One trick is to float a groundbait bowl in the top, allowing enough room at the edge to place a fish in the net when you catch one.

132

CHAPTER ELEVEN

BAITS AND GROUND-BAITS

There's nothing extra-special about the hook baits used for legering. They are the same as are used for any type of fishing. However, a quick-run-down on the more usual baits won't go amiss.

Maggots

Hook maggots and pinkies are most usually used on the hook, but squatts only rarely. The exceptions to this are in winter or when fishing for tiny fish in summer, when one or two squatts on a size 24 or size 26 may be necessary to get a bite. However, squatts are extremely useful for putting into cereal groundbait, as they are not a very active maggot and enable you to form good, solid balls of groundbait. Pinkies, on the other hand, are the worst type of maggot to use in balls of groundbait as they wriggle so much that they are very likely to break up the ball in mid-air. Pinkies can, however, be safely put into a groundbait feeder provided it can be pinched fairly solid for casting. Hook maggots can be put into cereal, and though not as active as pinkies they, also, can cause problems.

Squatts should normally be kept in the brown foundry sand in which they are sold, and it should be kept moist. You will be lucky to keep squatts for more than ten days in good condition, even in a refrigerator, while pinkies can be kept for weeks. Make sure that all maggots, particularly pinkies, are given plenty of air, as the heat they generate will condense on the lid of the maggot tin and block the holes, causing them to suffocate.

Hook maggots can last up to a couple of weeks if they are bought really fresh. Any left from one weekend's fishing are best used as casters the next weekend. Start riddling them on

133

the Wednesday ready for a Saturday, and keep them in sealed polythene bags in the refrigerator, taking out any old, floating ones from the first batch. Leave the rest of the maggots in a reasonably cool place and riddle them each morning and night, immediately putting the resulting casters in a sealed polythene bag in the refrigerator.

It is popular to colour maggots, although most tackle shops sell ready-coloured bait. Red and bronze are the most popular colours for hook maggots, with red and fluorescent pink the favourite for pinkies, and red for squatts. These are in addition to the natural colourings, of course.

One way of finding out which colour the fish prefer is to put three differently coloured maggots on one hook, and to check after a bite which has been marked. It's surprising how often this trick works. If the bait is too big for the fish to take an interest in, there is no alternative but to ring the changes by changing the colour each cast until you have found the one that the fish prefer.

It is possible to colour maggots yourself by buying a proprietory non-toxic dye. The secret is to make sure that the maggots are completely clean before you start. This can be done by immersing them in a sieve in warm water to get rid of any grease, and drying them as much as possible by shaking (not by adding any sort of maize meal or groundbait) before adding the dye. Then follow the instructions carefully.

Casters

These are a deadly bait for the leger and swimfeeder angler as they do not move, and so stay in position on the bottom better than maggots. Be sure not to use any casters that are going sour, as this will put fish off. Put into groundbait, casters are a favourite with bream anglers on stillwaters, while mixed with hemp in a swimfeeder they produce big catches of chub and barbel from fast rivers.

Some anglers like all their casters to be roughly the same colour, while others like a range of colours from light orange (the freshest ones) to dark brown. Probably more important is that they are fresh, and do not float. If they do float they will take fish out of your swim, especially on moving water.

Anglers using casters in groundbait, whether in balls or in an open-ended swimfeeder, often mix them with squatts, giving fish a choice of baits. Casters do not move at all, and squatts only a little, so you can get a lot into a handful of groundbait. However, in summer on some rivers it may be advisable not to use squatts because of the menace of eels!

Casters on the hook account for a lot of quality fish, and have the advantage that you can bury the hook right inside them. To do this, put the point against the blunt end, carefully pierce the skin, and turn the hook without breaking the side of the shell. Then tap down the spade end so it lodges inside the caster. The special long-shanked fine-wire hooks sold as caster hooks make this job easy. However, you should be wary of using these hooks for big fish as they can easily straighten on the strike.

As a general rule, the best casters to use as a hook bait are those which float. Not only are the shells harder, which makes it easy to bury the hook, but with the hook inside, their buoyancy makes them sink only slowly, similar to a normal sinking caster without a hook in it. Hook sizes for this are usually an 18 or a 16, though if you get big maggots and turn them slowly so that they do not lose much of their original size, it is possible to use a size 14 in a single caster without bursting it.

For carp in shallow waters, two or three floating casters on a size 12 hook are often sufficient, when fished with a long tail, to keep the bait floating on the surface, where you can see the carp take them. The larger the hook, the heavier it is, of course, so you may, find that it is necessary to add a pinch of bread flake to keep the bait floating. Carp will still take the bait as it is sinking, so don't worry too much about whether it stays on the surface.

Bread

Bread flake and bread paste are both deadly baits for most species. Flake is made by scraping out a piece of fresh bread about the size of a fingernail, and putting it on the hook in one of two ways. Easiest is to double the flake around the hook and pinch it just once round the top of the shank. Don't pinch it all round the hook, as new bread will go hard in the water if pinched, and apart from not being fluffy and attractive, this will inhibit the strike. Alternatively, you can lightly pinch the piece in the middle, and put the point of the hook through this. It is important to match the size of the hook to the size of the bread flake, as it swells in water. Rarely should you use less than a size 14 or a size 12 with bread flake. This entails using a hook length of 2 lb or 3 lb, so it's not a method you can switch to quickly if you're using normal light tackle – you'll need a spare leger rod made up with heavier line.

Bread paste can be made in any size. And you can use it on a hook as small as a size 18, though since it would usually be used to tempt bigger fish, a size 14 or larger would be usual. To make paste take some old bread, without the crusts. Wet it well, and knead it in an old cloth, squeezing out as much of the water as you can. Then mould it all round the hook so that the point is just about covered. New bread is not good for

135

Above: Redworms and brandlings. The brandlings have the yellow stripes round them.

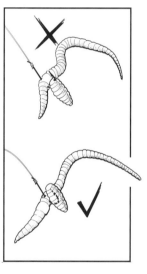

Worm and caster 'cocktails' are a deadly bait for bream. Top: don't hook a worm through its saddle, as this is its softest part. Bottom: hook it above or below the band. Another trick is to leave the hook point inside the caster so it doesn't catch on bottom-growing weed.

136

making paste as it goes too sticky and hard. Paste is a brilliant bait for bream, while flavoured with cheese it is a classic bait for chub.

Worms

In a flood, lobworms are a good standby, and are now a standard bait even with match anglers on rivers like the Trent, where they take chub when fished right in the margins. The tail of a lobworm is also a good bait for big roach in summer, especially at dusk. Collect lobs on warm, dewy evenings after dark, when you will see them lying on the lawn, or on the earth in a flowerbed or border. You'll have to search for them with a torch, and trap them by putting pressure on them at the point where they enter the hole. A slow, steady pull will bring them out of the hole. Beware, because they are extremely sensitive to footfalls, and can retract at lightning speed into the hole. Keep them in a tin with some grass and just a little earth, but don't keep any damaged ones, as the others will quickly die. Lobworms don't keep well in a small container, and generally it's better to gather them for each trip, letting the others go.

Redworms and brandlings are very similar, and are an excellent bait for eels (unfortunately), bream, perch and most other species, including tench. They are smaller than the large lobworm, and brandlings are distinguished by yellow rings round their bodies. On the whole, redworms are considered by many anglers to be the better bait for most species, but both will take fish. Redworms are the worms you will find under sacking that has been lying in the garden. However, by far the best place to look for them is on an established compost heap to which fresh rubbish is regularly added, or on well-rotted manure heaps. Many anglers have a compost heap especially for worms. It should be supported around the edges so the top is flat, as a sloping top will tend to drain the rain off and the heap will not become wet enough for the worms to inhabit it.

The best type of compost is made in a big plastic drum or a fertiliser bag. You will need some worms, bought or borrowed, to start the cycle. Put them into some partly rotted compost (a mixture of earth and soft vegetable matter will do if you don't have any rotted matter) in the bottom of the drum or bag, and keep adding fresh vegetable matter, ensuring that it is either watered regularly or kept open to the rain and watered in hot weather. Try to disturb the worms as little as possible for a few months, until they are well established, and when you see masses of tiny white worms, you will know they are breeding. The compost can be kept in a garage without creating a smell provided you avoid putting any

A good tip for adding water to groundbait – use an inverted maggot tin.

meat, which will rot and attract flies, in the bag. Newspapers are good (they should be wetted first), as are scraps of cooked vegetables from the table (the worms find cooked matter easier to digest than fresh leaves), old lettuce leaves potato peelings, marrows and fruit. Almost any soft vegetable matter will do except rhubarb sticks or leaves. Avoid adding large amounts of grass cuttings if possible, as these can stop the matter underneath from rotting. If you have the moisture content right, the worms will be lying near the surface and you won't have to dig much to find them.

Redworms and brandlings will keep for weeks in a maggot tin, but will quickly lose their size and become weak and limp if not fed regularly. You should return them every fortnight or so to the compost and take out some fresh ones. When you take some for fishing, you must take plenty of compost with them, as they need it to keep moist. Don't leave the container in a car boot in very hot weather or the worms will die as I found to my cost when I went to Holland one summer! Within two days there was nothing left of them.

Generally, a single redworm should be hooked near the

137

head. It's best to avoid the thick saddle or ring near the head as this tends to be soft. For a bunch of worms, hook them once through the middle. If you have trouble hooking a worm, roll it on your knee under your fingers for a couple of seconds. It will relax sufficiently long to allow you to get the hook in.

Luncheon meat

This is an excellent bait for many species, and is used mainly on fast water for chub and barbel and on stillwaters for carp. Cut it into cubes before going fishing. To toughen the cubes so they stay on the hook better lightly grill them for a couple of minutes, or microwave for 20–30 seconds, or leave them exposed to the air overnight. On stillwaters it's easy to groundbait with the cubes, as they can be catapulted in. On fast water you should check to see whether the cubes float; a high fat content will cause them to do this. If they don't sink well, use some in a large, open-ended feeder plugged with groundbait at each end in order to get them into the swim. That way they get to the bottom more quickly. You'll need a size 10 hook or larger to use meat properly. If you have trouble hooking the meat, push the hook, bend first, through the middle of the cube, turn the hook through 90° and pull it back. Alternatively, you can push the bend through to the other side and insert a tiny piece of dried grass under the bend to stop the hook being pulled back through the meat.

Sweetcorn

Sweetcorn is an extremely useful bait on all waters, especially now that many anglers are using it and fish have become used to eating it. The beauty is that it's bought ready to use, though some water-owners ban tins and poythene bags on the bank, and you may need to empty the contents into a bait tin before you start. Hook sizes are 14 or 12 for a single grain, or a size 10 or larger for two or more grains. If there are big fish in the water, you can thread several grains right up the shank to hide the hook. Sweetcorn can be catapulted out into still or slow-moving water, or put into a groundbait feeder for faster water.

Bloodworm

Although thought of primarily as a pole angler's bait, some top-line anglers regularly leger with a bunch of bloodworms. The smaller jokers are mixed in a proprietory brand of groundbait and put into the swim in balls, or in a groundbait feeder, in the same way as squatts and casters. You can work a lot into a small amount of groundbait as they are comparatively inactive.

Groundbait

The principle of mixing groundbait is covered in Chapter 8. All groundbait should be mixed in the same way – by mixing the ingredients well first, then by adding water to the groundbait, never the other way round. If you stir the water in quickly, this ensures that no one portion of the groundbait becomes any wetter than the rest, and helps ensure its consistency. A round bowl is recommended because there are no corners in which any dry groundbait can get trapped, it all mixes up properly. For a groundbait feeder, special groundbaits are sold that are mixed fairly dry and then 'explode' from the feeder, making an attractive cloud, as used in the lake swim in Chapter 9. For putting groundbait in by hand, you will usually need it slightly wetter. Always add the water in tiny amounts.

For deep-water swims such as on the Fens or slow rivers, where you need the groundbait to break open only on the bottom, perhaps when you are after bream, you have to make the balls good and solid, by adding more water. Use a commercial groundbait that clearly states it is for deep waters, and add white breadcrumbs to stiffen it even further if necessary. A good trick is to add an additive that largely consists of crushed hempseed. This does not readily absorb water, and when you have put in a ball containing this, you can see the tiny particles rising and breaking the surface. Not only does this attract the fish, but it tells you exactly where your groundbait is.

Of course, not all leger anglers want groundbait to go directly to the bottom, in which case mix less water to make it drier, or more water to make it sloppy. Both will break up before the balls hit bottom, but you can throw very sloppy groundbait only a short distance, and only underarm, so it's rarely used by leger anglers. If you are using dry or sloppy groundbait, you should be using a rig that allows the bait to drop slowly, of course. If you are using a heavy groundbait, you have a choice between using a short tail to get the bait down quickly, or using a long tail to give a natural fall. On the whole you will be better off on stillwaters if you allow a long drop to begin with.

You are advised to hit on a basic mixture of groundbait and stick to it until you can mix it perfectly. For most purposes, it's right when you can pick up a handful and squeeze it once, and find it binds together but breaks apart soon after you drop it in the water. Squeezing it harder will make it more solid, and squeezing it less will make it break up more quickly. For bream it's important to get the groundbait out in one ball, whether thrown in by hand or put in with a catapult. The worst thing is for the ball to break apart before it hits the

139

Use a round bowl for mixing groundbait in.

water. If you have a lot of maggots or casters in the groundbait, it must be good and solid to hold together properly. First settle on your perfect mix. Then – and only then – should you start experimenting with additives or other groundbaits.

The top French anglers mix their groundbait the night before a match to allow it to absorb all the water, and just add a little more water if necessary in the morning, and you can do worse than try this if you have trouble mixing groundbait on the bank. If you mix it on the bank you should spend at least five minutes stirring it, though too few anglers do this. If you are throwing a ball a long way, always wet your hands just before throwing it, as described in the Chapter 8 and mould the ball in your palms. This makes the surface smoother and more solid, keeping the ball together and making the throwing more accurate.

A groundbait pattern for bream anglers

It's always useful to have a plan when you target a specific species like bream, as it can be dificult to know where to put your groundbait, especially on a river, canal or Fen drain. The bream will probably be moving along the far bank parallel to the shore, but will refuse to move more than 1–2 ft from their chosen route. Books give all sorts of groundbaiting patterns – boxes or stars are popular. However, for the angler who is undecided, the safest pattern is probably along a diagonal line, starting opposite you and close in to the far bank, and moving downstream, or downwind, to a point 20 ft out from the bank. The diagram shows the exact pattern, which is the simplest possible, and which ensures that at some point the patrolling fish will find the groundbait.

This pattern enables you to start legering at the far bank, with no chance of bringing your leger tackle back through the shoal. You can roll or work a light leger downstream and since it will move out from the bank a little every time you move it, this will roughly follow the line of groundbait. Always fish between you and the line of groundbait, only going on to the groundbait or past it when you are desperate. Once the fish are in residence try, at all costs, to avoid hooking a fish on or beyond the groundbait line, and try to avoid letting a hooked fish swim into the shoal. This pattern gives you a better chance of doing this than any other.

Catapults

Modern catapults allow you to put out golfball-sized balls of groundbait to 50 yd or more. Take care not to mix in too many maggots or casters, as the force when the ball is

You can put groundbait out 50 yd or more using one of the new specially-made groundbait catapults.

Bream tend to patrol the far bank of many waters. This groundbait pattern should ensure they find your bait. But always fish on the near side of the band of groundbait.

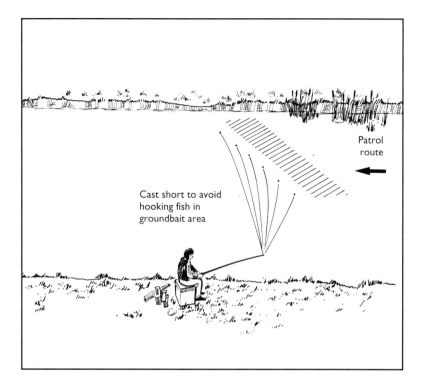

Patrol route

Cast short to avoid hooking fish in groundbait area

released helps break it apart. If you mould the ball with wet handsbefore putting it in the catapult, this may help.

It's important to hold the catapult correctly. If you are right-handed your right arm should be extended fully, and if your wrists are strong you may be able to steady the catapult with your thumb braced behind it. If you have difficulty doing this with a powerful catapult you will have to grip the handle tightly with your full clenched fist. The left hand holds the cup somewhere around your left ribs, and the release should be clean, without any noticeable flexing of the right arm. Ideally you should have two or three catapults, each tensioned differently, so you use each one to its maximum capacity to get the required distance – in the same way that a golfer swings each club with the same amount of force, with the face angle of each iron determining the distance the balls goes.

Don't neglect to loose-feed when legering. You will rarely be fishing close enough to throw bait in by hand, but you will often be close enough to use a loose-feed catapult. Indeed, if you can loose-feed a swim containing big fish you will usually be better off doing so, as the splash of the groundbait, while being ignored by many small fish, can upset the larger specimens, particularly bream. If the wind makes it difficult, and is causing the loose-feed to fall short of its intended target, then resort to groundbait. At least it will get your bait out there.